the new
Photo Crafts

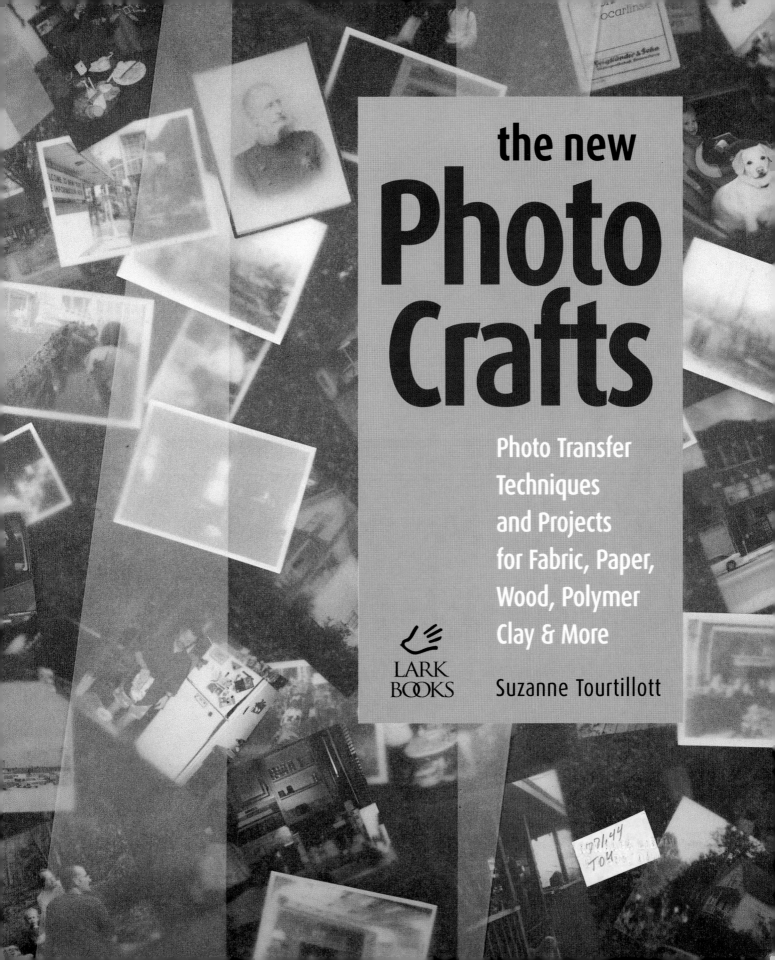

the new
Photo
Crafts

Photo Transfer
Techniques
and Projects
for Fabric, Paper,
Wood, Polymer
Clay & More

LARK
BOOKS

Suzanne Tourtillott

CHRIS BRYANT
art director

EVAN BRACKEN
photography

HANNES CHAREN
illustrations
production assistance

VERONIKA ALICE GUNTER
NICOLE TUGGLE
assistant editors

in the memory of
MORRIS RUDY MONTGOMERY

Library of Congress Cataloging-in-Publication Data

Tourtillot, Suzanne J.E.
     The new photocrafts : photo transfer techniques and projects for fabric, paper, wood, polymer clay and more / Suzanne J.E. Tourtillot.
        p.   cm.
     Includes index.
     ISBN 1-57990-203-0 (pbk.)
     1. Photographs—Triming, mounting, etc.   2. Handicraft.   I. Title

  TR340.T68 2001
  771'.44—dc21   00-059518
                                                 CIP
10 9 8 7 6 5 4 3 2

Published by Lark Books, a division of
Sterling Publishing Co., Inc.
387 Park Avenue South
New York, N.Y. 10016

© 2001, Lark Books

Distributed in Canada by Sterling Publishing,
c/o Canadian Manda Group, One Atlantic Ave., Suite 105
Toronto, Ontario, Canada M6K 3E7

Distributed in Australia by Capricorn Link (Australia) Pty Ltd.,
P.O.Box 704, Windsor, NSW 2756 Australia

Distributed in the U.K. by Guild of Master Craftsman Publications Ltd.,
Castle Place 166 High Street, Lewes, East Sussex, England, BN7 1XU.
Tel: (+44) 1273 477374 • Fax: (+44) 1273 478606
Email: pubs@thegmcgroup.com • Web: www.gmcpublications.com

The written instructions, photographs, designs, patterns, and projects in this volume are intended for the personal use of the reader and may be reproduced for that purpose only. Any other use, especially commercial use, is forbidden under law without written permission of the copyright holder.

Every effort has been made to ensure that all the information in this book is accurate. However, due to differing conditions, tools, and individual skills, the publisher cannot be responsible for any injuries, losses, and other damages that may result from the use of the information in this book.

If you have questions or comments about this book, please contact:
Lark Books
67 Broadway
Asheville, North Carolina 28801
828-236-9730

Printed in China

All rights reserved

ISBN 1-57990-203-0

18.95

CONTENTS

INTRODUCTION

Have you ever looked at old family photos and been completely charmed by the happy marriage of familiar faces and historical detail you saw there? Great-grandpa standing by his Model "T," the cameo brooch gleaming in Aunt Harriet's wedding portrait, even those awful polka-dotted pedalpushers from seventh grade—priceless now! They all have one thing in common: they remind us of the oft-forgotten little details; they round out our memories of the past. And whether it's the triumph of a first step, a new home, or just the satisfaction of a really great mud pie, the photos we're snapping today will someday tell our stories for us.

When you look at it that way, photography plays an important part in all our lives. Did Thanksgiving dinner ever really begin before a picture of the table and everyone around it had been taken? What did the swimsuit look like that your mother wore when she was four? Usually it's the photographs that tell the tale, long after we are gone. And photographs, when they are meaningfully made, get passed down through the generations, linking us, one to another: this nose, that chin…your first bicycle-riding lesson.

Most of us have accumulated albums, framed photos, and envelopes bulging with prints from years past. This book shows you how to use photographs and photographic imagery in ways you may have never thought of before. We'll introduce you to many different craft techniques that use photography in one way or another, and that's what makes this book very different from most other craft books. The projects range in skill level from simple to advanced, but everything you need to know to try a new craft material or technique is right here.

It's exciting to realize you can do so much with the piles
and boxes of pictures you've been accumulating over the
years. These photos may get new life through a decorative handcoloring technique, or be totally transformed
onto a box or a light switch! We hope you'll find all the
projects interesting and challenging, and that they'll
stimulate you to invent new craft projects of your own,
once you know the possibilities.

Some of the projects use the actual snapshots you have
at home, and others need to be reproduced on a color or
a black-and-white photocopier. There are even projects
that recycle both "reject" pictures and uncut film from
the movie theater! We haven't forgotten the digital rev-
olution, either. A majority of us now own home computers that came packaged with some basic imaging
software—we can't possibly leave out that option. This
book covers techniques and technologies from the 19th
to the 21st centuries; we hope you'll find inspiration on
every page. We'll also suggest some easy ways you can
improve your skills as a photographer, even if you're
using a disposable or a point-and-shoot camera. And if
you're thinking digitally, read on. A complete discussion
about filmless photography (let's coin the term "digitography") and all things pixelated comes later.

Before moving on to the craft projects themselves, we'd
like to make a few suggestions about how you can take
better pictures. Feel free to skip this section, if you like.
Then, once you've been introduced to the craft techniques you'll need to produce the exciting projects in
this book, it's time to get going! The numbers and facts
may need to percolate for awhile, but don't let that hold
you back from having a wonderful time trying new
things. And don't forget to look for beauty and inspiration in the everyday.

SEEING AND SHOOTING

"THE PHOTOGRAPHER IS LIKE THE COD, WHICH LAYS A MILLION EGGS IN ORDER THAT ONE MAY BE HATCHED."

GEORGE BERNARD SHAW (1856–1950), FAMOUS DRAMATIST AND WIT

Shaw must have felt the frustration we've all experienced when the shot didn't "turn out." Taking better photographs can be a fun and rewarding hobby—despite the disappointments—once you learn something about shooting, lighting, and composition. There are many models of 35 millimeter cameras from which to choose, each with its pros and cons, but using your camera to its fullest capacity and knowing the qualities of the light you have to work with are basic tools available to anyone, and they are essential for making successful pictures.

TOP: 35 mm point-and-shoot camera

RIGHT: Kodak advertisement, 1908

If it isn't an Eastman, it isn't a Kodak.

The Kodak Girl.

'Tis **Kodak Simplicity**

and Kodak film convenience that have made pocket photography possible. Not only does the Kodak go inside the pocket, but inside the Kodak goes the film—all becomes one compact, self-contained mechanism.

Kodaks, $5 to $75.

A new folding Kodak for the pocket—almost for the vest pocket, at $6.00.

EASTMAN KODAK CO.

Catalogue at the dealers Rochester, N. Y. *or by mail.*

$2,000 in prizes for the best Kodak and Brownie Pictures.

POINT-AND-SHOOT: THE EASY OPTION

A point-and-shoot camera makes most of your technical decisions for you. It has preset focus- and flash-ranges, calculates the exposure according to the film speed you're using, and usually has a built-in flash. It is simple to operate, and people who like to take spontaneous snaps with a minimum of fuss enjoy using it for precisely these reasons. Some models are so feature-loaded that their prices rival those of the moderately priced interchangeable-lens cameras, with zoom lenses and a choice of film formats built right in.

With the disposable 35 millimeter camera, picture taking is as easy as pressing a button. Disposables are actually very much like the first simple cameras for amateurs that appeared in 1888 when the Eastman Kodak Company promised that if "You Press The Button, We Do The Rest." Today you can choose an outdoor-only model, or one with a built-in flash, in a variety of film speeds (see Film Facts, page 12, for more information). They're small and light and great for all sorts of surprise situations, so keep more than one kind handy. You'll definitely need to stay within the limits of the near-focus and flash ranges. Just don't get too close, or the flash exposure and focus won't be right. The information will be printed right on the box or package. Look for special-purpose designs, too, like a longer, "portrait" lens, a panoramic format, or a water-resistant model.

THE 35 MILLIMETER CAMERA SYSTEM

This type of camera is often referred to as a *system*, because everything is designed and built to work together in a dedicated fashion. It uses interchangeable lenses, and usually offers even more automated features than the point-and-shoot; autofocus and auto-film frame advance help you keep up with fast-moving situations. Go ahead and override the automatic features as your confidence level builds.

The adjustable-focus lens allows for more creative expression; you can focus within inches of your subject, isolate it from a sea of distracting details, or zoom in from 30 feet (9 m) away. Photographs taken with a wide-angle lens usually have a generous, spacious look, great for capturing the "feel" of a landscape or the town square, and a longer lens is perfect for closeup portraits. Zoom lenses, however, are the most versatile—like having several different lenses combined in a single, neat package.

TOP: **35 mm interchangeable-lens camera**

RIGHT: Wes and Will enjoying watermelon. Keep your subject within the preset focus- and flash-ranges of a point-and-shoot camera. *Photo by Dawn Cusick*

GETTING BETTER RESULTS FROM NATURAL LIGHT AND AUTOFLASH

One of the most common reasons for an unsatisfactory photograph is its lighting—or lack of it. Red-eye, wildly "off" color, and bleached faces are common disappointments for the snapshooter. No matter what kind of camera equipment you use, your basic lighting tools are the sun and sky, and the electronic flash unit. Taking advantage of sunlight's best qualities and effectively using the flash are easy when you follow a few sensible guidelines.

Bright sunlight caused Wes to squint.
Photo by Dawn Cusick

Grendel's dark fur needed fill flash to adjust the balance between the shadows and bright sunlight.
Photo by Paige Gilchrist

Using the Sun and the Sky

Perhaps you remember when it was very important to carefully position yourself and your camera with your back to the sun. This made sure your subject was well-lit, but a smile usually turned into a squint. Back then, a good exposure could only be made in the brightest possible light. And there's no doubt that bright, sunny days are still great for showing off strong color and crisp detail. When photographing people, however, try using *open shade* instead. In it, the light falling on the subject is reflected by a clear sky from mid-morning until mid-afternoon. You're in open shade when you're shaded from the sun, but you can still see the clear sky overhead. The shady side of a building is fine, but the deep shadows under big trees won't work as well, because the light from the sky is filtered too much by the trees themselves. A light overcast sky also works well for many photographs; harsh shadows are gone, since they're filled in by the soft, diffuse light. Either sort of light, open shade or overcast, is flattering—and comfortable—for everyone.

Electronic Flash

A built-in flash can be used wisely—even creatively—if these few pointers are kept in mind. When using flash, don't point the camera straight at windows, mirrors, and other reflective surfaces. Keep your subjects several feet away from walls and the like, so that the light from the flash can fall on the ground behind them; then you won't end up with distracting, gloomy shadows in the shot.

The better models of auto-everything cameras offer a choice of several flash modes. One really useful feature is the fill flash mode. Use it outdoors (even when you think you might not need it) to better capture a darker or shadowed subject in an otherwise well-lit scene. Finally, it's important to remember that a flash is designed to work best within a predetermined distance range based on how powerful the unit is; anything outside this range will be either overexposed (too light) or underexposed (too dark). Red-eye is a problem when the subject directly faces the flash unit in a low-light situation; certain 35 millimeter camera designs have an anti–red-eye feature as part of the built-in flash.

BE KIND TO YOUR CAMERA

Photographic equipment and materials are as subject to damage from heat, dust, and humidity as any other piece of electronic equipment. Take as much care with your camera and films as you do for any other electronic device. Turn to Protect Your Memories, page 16, for more tips on storing prints and negatives.

FRAMING AND CROPPING YOUR SUBJECT

Whatever your choice of camera, it is you, the photographer, who has the final word on how your shots turn out. Consider how far away you are from your subject, and how you will hold the camera, because distance and orientation make a big impact on the final look of the photograph. Do you always seem to take your pictures from the same distance? Move a few steps closer, but not too close. Fixed-focus (point-and-shoot and disposable) cameras require that you stay at least 3 feet (.9 m) away.

Most of us have been surprised to see all sorts of things in the final photograph that we didn't notice when we were taking it. For a strong and simple picture, especially for portraits, stand 4 to 6 feet (1.2 to 1.8 m) from your subject. Look for a background that won't compete for the center of attention—pleasing colors and simple shapes make for a background that lets the subject speak for itself. For subjects at or near the ground, such as children, pets, and flowers, kneel to their level for a really effective snapshot.

There are plenty of times when you want your picture to tell a bigger story: who, what, where, when, and why. The basic picture elements of foreground, point of focus, and background help do this. The foreground is everything in the picture that is closer than your subject. Trees, paths, and all kinds of interesting details at the edges of the picture, and in front of the main subject, add real depth to the image. The main subject doesn't have to be in the center of the shot, either. Try shifting the camera so the subject isn't exactly in the middle, but instead just a bit to the left

This snapshot of Margaret was taken at her eye level.
Photo by Michael C. Murphy

or right side. The background establishes a stage, so to speak, for the actors to play upon—whether they're in a parking lot or a park. Make an effort to leave out the trash cans and telephone poles (unless they're part of what you want your picture to say), and you'll probably be happier with the results. Cameras can be held vertically as well as horizontally. Is your scene long and low, or taller than it is wide? Just taking a moment to turn the camera to better match your subject's orientation can really change the way your picture looks, and you'll be better able to capture only what you want in the shot.

FILM FACTS

Choices and still more choices… should it be color, black-and-white, mail order, or one-hour? And what about film numbers, and "indoor" film compared to "outdoor" film? You don't have to have an expert at your elbow; learning a few important facts about film will give you satisfying results and fewer disappointments.

WHICH FILM IS RIGHT?

Not all film is created equal, and that's why there are so many of them. Each one has its advantages and its drawbacks, and for most people, it's not as important which brand you choose as it is what speed is right for the kind of pictures you want to take. A good, general rule of thumb is, the lower the ISO (International Standards Organization) number, the more light you'll need when taking pictures. This number is often referred to as the film's "speed." The higher the number, for instance, the more the amount of light can vary from shot to shot, and the better you'll be able to "freeze" moving subjects, too. ISO ratings of 400 and up indicate a versatile film that lets you move with confidence between a foggy, early morning scene and bright, midday subjects. If you don't know what kind of light you'll be shooting in, buy an ISO 400 film.

Slower films, such as ISO 100 to 200, yield crisp pictures with sharp detail, but you'll need to have plenty of light for all your shots—either with flash, or in bright outdoor scenes, such as snowy landscapes, or at the beach. What you gain is the better detail that is needed for bigger enlargements, such as 8 x 10's, without sacrificing sharpness. But beware: some point-and-shoot cameras are meant to perform well with only one speed of film, usually ISO 400.

Camera shops usually offer a wider choice of films than do larger chain outlets, and they can help you choose the right film for your needs. If you're buying black-and-white film, find out what kind of processing it will need. Special black-and-white films, called "chromogenics," can be processed and printed in quick-lab color chemistry, but most other black-and-white films cannot. Use chromogenic film when you want to get it developed and printed in a hurry. And even though traditional black-and-white film requires special processing, most towns have a local lab that can handle it. The quick labs will ship it off for developing, so either way, you'll probably have to wait several days (at least) to see your results.

FILM PROCESSING

All photo processors provide basic services, such as film developing and printing. You might choose one because it's convenient to home or work, but when it comes to services and supplies, there are more options than ever. Some shops have club memberships that give discounts to repeat customers. With mail order you trade instant gratification for greater savings. A growing number of the big chains not only develop and print your film but will also turn your pictures into downloadable digital files or a CD-ROM for you to use on your home computer, and e-mail you some web-ready pictures, too.

Extra prints are inexpensive when they're made at the time the film is processed. Ask for doubles, or even triples, of each print, and shop around for the best price. You'll want plenty of duplicate prints to make the Sailor's Vintage Print Quilt on page 23. The Zany Zigzagged Film Frame, on the next page, is a standout way to recycle uncut film from the processors, and they'll be happy to let you take some from their recycling bin.

Zany Zigzagged Film Frame

DESIGNER: **POLLY HARRISON**

If you made long, zigzag chains from chewing gum wrappers as a child, then this project will bring back pleasant memories. Use color negatives for a warm amber color, and black-and-white ones for cool gray and black. It's easy to get uncut 35 millimeter film from the photo processor. Schools and libraries are an excellent source for out-of-date filmstrips, and movie theaters sometimes discard their "trailers," instead of returning them to the distributors.

Materials

35 mm film negatives or
filmstrips, cut to size as
described below

Inexpensive 8 x 10-inch
(20.25 x 25.5 cm)
picture frame

Tools

Ruler

Scissors

Bone folder

Hot glue gun and glue sticks,
or glue suitable for plastic

Instructions

Ask the clerk at the photo processor
for uncut negative film from their
recycling bin. If you're using film
from the photo processor, you'll
need twelve 24-exposure or nine 36-
exposure rolls, or enough film for
thirty-two 12-inch (30.5 cm) strips.

1 Measure and cut thirty-two
12-inch (30.5 cm) lengths of
35 mm film. Make sure the ends are
cut straight at a 90-degree angle.

2 Fold a strip in half, then fold
each end inward to the first fold
(see figure 1). Use the side of the
bone folder to make sharp creases.

3 Fold and crease the remaining
strips in the same way and set
them aside.

4 Hold two units, one in each
hand, by the single fold so that
the two folded ends point upward.
Insert the two folds of the right unit
into the two folds of the left unit,
and push the unit in the right hand
up to the top of the two folds in the
left unit. Hold the single fold in
your left hand and pull the two
snugly, so they are at right angles to
each other (see figure 2).

5 Working on a flat surface, insert
another unit into the two folds
that are open, creating a zigzag
shape, as in figure 3. Continue until
you have used nine units.

6 After inserting the ninth unit,
insert the tenth unit down to
the right. This will end the zigzag
with a square shape (see figure 4).

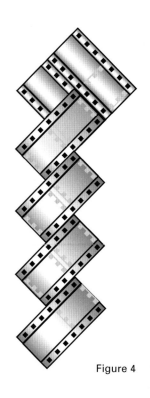

Figure 4

7 Insert a unit in the usual man-
ner up into the unit that made
the square. Add five additional units
across, as you did in step 5.

8 Make another square corner by
inserting a unit down to the left.

9 Work down eight units, turn
the corner with a unit, and then
work across five units (see figure 5).

Figure 1

Figure 2

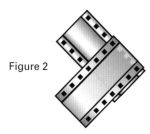

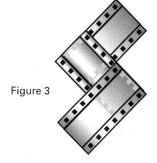
Figure 3

11 Use hot glue, or any suitable adhesive, to apply the film frame to your purchased frame. Apply the adhesive in a zigzag line on the back of the film, about $\frac{1}{2}$ inch (1.3 cm) from the inside edge. Position the film over the frame and press down until it adheres. Dry under a heavy weight.

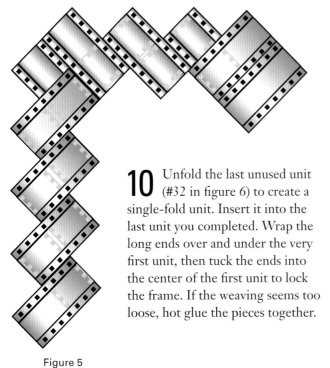

10 Unfold the last unused unit (#32 in figure 6) to create a single-fold unit. Insert it into the last unit you completed. Wrap the long ends over and under the very first unit, then tuck the ends into the center of the first unit to lock the frame. If the weaving seems too loose, hot glue the pieces together.

Figure 5

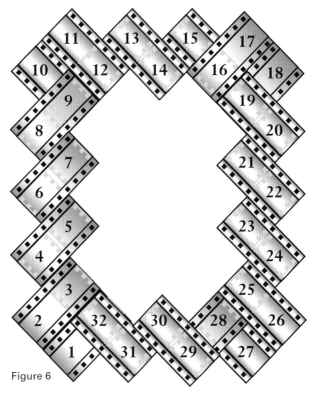

Figure 6

CRAFTING WITH PHOTOGRAPHIC PRINTS

"THE VERY THINGS WHICH AN ARTIST WOULD LEAVE OUT, OR RENDER IMPERFECTLY, THE PHOTOGRAPH TAKES INFINITE CARE WITH, AND SO RENDERS ITS ILLUSIONS PERFECT."

OLIVER WENDELL HOLMES (1809–1904), POET, ESSAYIST, AND PHYSICIAN

Photographic prints are rather delicate creatures. They are subject to damage over time from ordinary conditions, such as the ultraviolet wavelength present in sunlight, the changing levels of humidity, and even the oil from your skin. Prints are not easily cleaned, but they are all too easily scratched. When you're handling vintage photos (especially those without the original negative), handle them only by the edges.

IS IT A PRINT OR AN IMAGE?

You're going to encounter two terms over and over again in this book. Let us explain the difference between "print" and "image" right now: The pictures you pick up from the photofinisher we call *prints*. The picture on the print, however, can be transferred to another surface; this we'll call an *image*. For example, a photo of your child is a print, but when it's photocopied or transferred to fabric, it becomes an image.

PROTECT YOUR MEMORIES

If you're serious about protecting all your photographs from the ravages of time, don't store your prints or negatives using ordinary wood-pulp papers or polyvinylchloride plastics. These materials are often used in the manufacture of inexpensive photo albums, and they slowly release acids and gases that stain, stick, and mar your pictures over time. The harmful plastics have a strong, chemical odor that indicates their toxic nature. Store and display both your negatives and prints using only archival, acid-free materials, which are becoming more widely available. The terms "archival" and "acid free" indicate plastics, papers, inks, and other materials that can be safely used for long-term contact with negatives and prints (they are pH neutral, or slightly alkaline).

Be sure to keep your negatives and any vintage photos that have no negatives as safe as any string of pearls or stock certificates, and consider a fireproof box for the truly irreplaceable items. To protect framed prints exposed to daylight, use UV-filtering acrylic sheets, instead of glass. You can purchase these materials through mail-order companies devoted exclusively to archival storage and display materials of all types; their cost will be lower with quantity purchases.

COPY NEGATIVES
AND REPRINTS

Every photograph once had a negative—except instant-print film, of
course—but most old photographs
have long since become separated
from their orginal negatives. When
using old family photos for craft
projects, always opt to have a modern print made from the negative
rather than using the original. If no
negative is available, a copy negative will solve the problem. A full-
service photo house can easily do
this and can even "restore" a picture that has minor damage by
retouching either the copy negative
or the copy print. Always have a
copy made from a high-quality
original print. It should be sharp,
well-exposed, and clean. If a print
or negative is dirty, leave it to the
pros to clean it; household cleaners
will certainly ruin it!

Full-service photographic labs
also make custom enlargements on
specialty papers, usually within a
few days. Ask for the print surface
appropriate to your needs. A glossy
surface makes the image look crisp
and holds detail well in photocopies. A matte finish fiber base is
good for all kinds of direct hand-
work, such the vibrant coloring
with oils seen in Harriet on the
Beach (page 35).

TOP: Vintage studio
portrait, c. 1915

LEFT: This copy print was
made by first photographing
the original print, to make
a copy negative. Then the
negative was enlarged and
printed on fiber base paper
suitable for handcoloring.

FAR LEFT: 35 mm copy negative

INDEX PRINTS
AND CONTACT SHEETS

Color film processors now provide a handy *index print* with your processed prints. These tiny images help you choose the ones you'd like to have reprinted. A similar sort of print made for black-and-white negatives is called a *contact sheet*. The Modern Miniature Pin (page 22) can be made with a part of a color print, or a single image cut from a black-and-white contact sheet.

There are many innovative ways you can display photos that don't involve the same old picture frame approach. The projects that follow will inspire you to show off your best shots whether you're at home or on the go.

BELOW: Index print

RIGHT: Contact sheet of black-and-white 35 mm negatives
Photos by Dana Irwin

Materials

Photo (or copy of photo, enlarged
   to suit your purpose)

Foam-core board

Spray mount adhesive for photos

Tools

Metal-edge ruler

Pencil

Craft knife and replacement blades

Electric handheld jigsaw
   with a fine-toothed blade

Snapshooter's Puzzle

DESIGNER: **TERRY TAYLOR**

Surprise and delight the object of your affection with a puzzle
made from an enlarged photographic print. Children will enjoy
seeing their own faces in this age-old entertainment. The pieces
of the puzzle can be as simple or complex as you choose.

Instructions

1 Select your photo. Instead of using an original
photo, use a copy print. With a copy print you can
crop the photograph to eliminate distracting details,
or you can have a small original enlarged. The
designer used an 8 x 10-inch (20 x 25 cm) copy print
for this project.

2 Use a pencil to mark a piece of foam-core board
measuring 8 x 10 inches (20 x 25 cm), or larger or
smaller as your photo requires.

3 Work on a surface suitable for cutting and use a
metal-edge ruler as a guide to cut the foam-core
board with the craft knife.

HINT: It is best to first make a shallow cut in the
foam-core board, and then cut it a second time,
rather than to try to make a single, deep cut. The
shallow cut will act as a guide that keeps your craft
knife from slipping and ensures a straighter edge.

4 Follow the manufacturer's instructions for using
the spray mount adhesive. Mount the photo on
the foam-core board as desired.

5 You can cut the puzzle by hand with a craft knife.
It is tedious work to do, but it can be done. Better
yet, use a small electric jigsaw (or any jigsaw with a
fine blade) to cut out the puzzle. Use long, curving
lines—either horizontally or vertically—then cut
those pieces again to make the puzzle pieces.

Anniversary Couple Commemorative Portrait

DESIGNER: **TERRY TAYLOR**

An original wedding portrait becomes a source of inspiration for a special wedding anniversary (here, the couple's sixth) when a few simple adornments are added to it.

Materials

Original or copy of wedding photo

2 hollow plastic columns 6 inches (15.25 cm) tall (find them in the wedding section of any craft store)

2 small bunches of wired ribbon flowers (again, the wedding section)

Foam-core board

Spray mount adhesive for photos

Toothpick or bamboo skewer

Precut wooden number

Silver or gold metallic-look paint

Tools

Craft knife and replacement blades

Hot glue gun and glue sticks

Electric handheld jigsaw with fine-toothed blade

Small paint brush

Craft drill with $1/16$-inch (1.5 mm) bit or awl

Instructions

1 Have an 8 x 10-inch (20.25 x 25.25 cm) copy negative and print made from the original photograph. You can crop it so that just the figures are enlarged, to get rid of extraneous details.

2 Position the photo on a piece of foam-core board large enough to fit the figures. Follow the manufacturer's instructions for using the spray adhesive, and mount the print on the board. Allow it to dry.

3 Use a craft knife to cut the figures away from the background. If you have access to a jigsaw, use it instead.

4 Create an easel-type stand by making a triangle from scrap foamcore board, with a $1\frac{1}{2}$-inch (3.75 cm) base and a 6-inch (15.25 cm) straight side. Cut it out with the craft knife.

5 Use hot glue to affix the easel stand to the back of the cutout.

6 Glue the base of each column to the front side of the cutout.

7 Fasten a bunch of small ribbon flowers to the inside top of each column with hot glue.

8 Paint the small wooden numeral with your choice of metallic paint.

9 Cut a $1\frac{1}{2}$ inch (3.75 cm) length of toothpick or bamboo skewer with a craft knife.

10 Use the craft drill or awl to make a shallow hole large enough for the toothpick or skewer to fit snugly in the back side of the wooden numeral.

11 Glue to attach the small stick to the numeral, then glue the stick to the cutout.

Modern Miniature Pin

DESIGNER: **PEGGY DEBELL**

Just as miniature portraitists once painted locket-size family pictures, you can create a tiny photo pin that will always be close to the heart. Whether it's a loved one, a pet, or a reminder of a favorite place, the print can be mounted easily in a simple, modern frame of decorated mat board.

Materials

Mat board (scrap may be purchased at your local framer)

Decorative papers

Contact sheet of black-and-white photos, or index print of color photos

White glue

Epoxy adhesive

Dimensional fabric paint, in assorted colors

Tools

Craft knife

Metal ruler

Scissors

$1\frac{1}{4}$-inch (6.25 mm) pin back

Instructions

1 If you're using a black-and-white photo, have the negatives made into a contact sheet at a photo shop (see Copy Negatives and Reprints, page 17), or cut a small part out of any copy or reprint—but never a vintage print.

2 Cut a piece of the mat board and a piece of the decorative paper about 4 x 4 inches (10 x 10 cm) square.

3 Use white glue to affix the decorative paper onto the mat board, and put a book or other heavy weight on top to keep them flat while drying. Let them dry thoroughly.

4 Cut two $1\frac{1}{2}$-inch (3.75 cm) squares out of the 4-inch (10 cm) square, using a sharp craft knife; use a metal ruler as a guide. Cut one of these squares in half diagonally, to make two triangles. Cut the rest of the board into strips about $\frac{1}{8}$-inch (3 mm) in width. You can use geometric shapes of any size that you like.

5 Cut out one of the photos on the contact sheet. Trim it down, so the long side is $\frac{3}{4}$ inch (2 cm) long. Glue it onto the $1\frac{1}{2}$-inch (3.75 cm) square. Place the photo under heavy weight until thoroughly dry.

6 Use white glue to attach the triangle to the right of the photo, and one of the strips on the left side. Let this dry. Add the other two strips to the top and bottom of the photo and again let it dry.

7 Using the epoxy glue, affix the pin back to the back side of the construction.

8 Use the dimensional paints to decorate the front of the pin by squeezing out small drops from the tube. Practice first on a scrap of paper to get the feel of how much pressure should be used.

Sailor's Vintage Print Quilt

DESIGNER: **ELLEN ZAHOREC**

This nautical wall hanging or "quilt" is made of a naval officer's original family photos from the 1950s. This project is a great way to recycle all those seagull and sunset pictures you took at the beach.

Materials

Narrow metallic tape, available from stained glass suppliers

Medium-weight canvas, cut to finished size (available at fabric stores)

2 or more large hook-and-eye closures

Tools

Zigzag sewing machine

Large safety pins

Instructions

If you don't want to use your original photos, have copies made. If the originals are small, the photo shop may agree to copy more than one onto the copy negative, which can save some money.

1 Lay out all the prints in a grid form to create an interesting pattern. These old photos are square, but rectangles work well, too.

2 Use contrasting or colorful thread and a wide zigzag stitch to sew the photos together, two at a time. Be sure to place the photos so that the edges butt up against one another. Do not overlap the photo edges; you want to be able to fold them back easily if you're doing a large design.

3 Sew these units together until you have enough for a row. Sew all the rows together.

4 Cut the lightweight canvas to the desired size, adding $2\frac{1}{2}$ inches (6.25 cm) to the measurement to allow for a hem.

5 Turn a $\frac{5}{8}$-inch (1.5 cm) hem around all the edges, and stitch it down using the sewing machine's regular straight stitch.

6 Lay the joined prints on top of the canvas, which will now have a $\frac{5}{8}$-inch (1.5 cm) border extending all around it. Carefully turn the canvas in, over the edges of the joined prints, and zigzag stitch the material on top of the prints' edges, forming a finished hem edge.

7 Lay down the metallic tape in a pleasing pattern on the borders, but not on the images themselves (see inset). Zigzag stitch over this, because the tape cannot adhere well to the thread and prints.

8 Measure and mark two places for the hanging hardware to be sewn onto the canvas back. The "eye" portion of the hook-and-eye closures will be used as hanging hardware. These small metal loops must be positioned far enough apart so the top edge and corners do not sag. To find the best placement for them, use safety pins first, to check that it will hang nicely.

9 Using a whipstitch, sew the eyes onto the canvas back with needle and thread. Do not pass the needle through the prints.

"Home is Where the Heart Is" Frame Magnets

DESIGNER: **CONNIE MATRICARDI**

Refrigerator magnets have a way of brightening up the kitchen. Your favorite snapshots of friends and family are always close by in these bright, creative frames.

Materials

Stiff paper or lightweight cardboard

1 sheet of red craft foam, 9 x 12 inches (22.75 x 30.5 cm)

1 sheet of purple craft foam, 9 x 12 inches (22.75 x 30.5 cm)

1 sheet of sturdy yellow craft felt, 9 x 12 inches (22.75 x 30.5 cm)

1 sheet of sturdy blue craft felt, 9 x 12 inches (22.75 x 30.5 cm)

1 sheet of sturdy red craft felt 3 x 3 inches (7.5 x 7.5 cm)

2 lengths of self-adhesive magnetic strip, 3 inches (7.5 cm) each

Snapshots

Tools

Scissors

Large foam brush or paintbrush

White craft glue

Air-soluble marker

Instructions

1 Enlarge the patterns 200 percent on a photocopier. Use stiff paper or cardboard to cut out patterns for the heart, the house, the circle, and the square. Using these patterns as a template, create another heart and house pattern slightly larger than the first.

2 Place the paper patterns for the hearts and houses on the appropriate felt or foam colors. Trace around the patterns with an air-soluble marker. Carefully cut out the felt or foam shapes.

3 Place the paper pattern for the circle on the red foam heart. Place the paper pattern for the square on the yellow felt house. Trace around the circle and square shapes with the marker. Carefully cut out these center shapes.

4 Cut a small heart out of the red felt piece, and glue it to the house, above the cutout opening.

5 Position each of the frames over the snapshots. If necessary, trim the photographs.

6 Position the snapshots between the front and back frame pieces, and glue them together.

7 Affix the magnetic strips to the back of each frame.

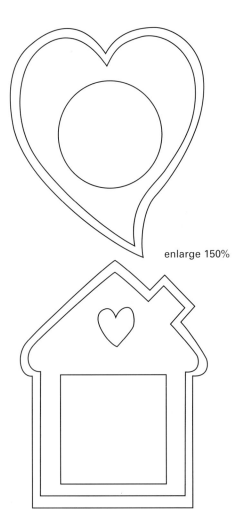

enlarge 150%

Convertible Star Book

DESIGNER: **DANIEL ESSIG**

This portable star book holds snapshots in nesting concertinas that convert into a lovely star-shaped diorama. A diorama is a miniature, three-dimensional scene that features a subject in a nature setting. If you like to take a lot of pictures on your outings, you may want to combine landscapes with portraits and closeups; each scene uses three photographic prints.

Instructions

1 Select five sets of three 4 x 6-inch (10 x 15.25 cm) photographic prints: one for the horizontal background; one for the middle ground (this is usually where the main subject is); and one for the foreground. Only part of each of the middle ground and foreground photos will be used, so choose them with this in mind. Since the prints will nest inside one another, each is cut to a slightly smaller length, but all of them are 4 inches (10 cm) high. Although these book structures are simple and involve very little sewing, designing your diorama takes careful planning, practice, and a little patience.

The concertina is made from the durable paper by folding it, accordion-style, and leaving a tail at each end. Be sure to cut the paper so that the grain runs across the 4-inch (10 cm) height of each piece; this allows for crisp folds (see Finding the Grain of the Paper, page 77). The concertinas are slightly larger than the largest print, leaving a 1/2-inch (1.25 cm) tail at each end of the concertina and 1/8-inch border all around the prints. This makes the sewing easier, because the stitching will then pass through these areas, rather than through the photos themselves.

2 The concertina that will hold the background pictures measures 4 x 29¾ inches (10 x 75.75 cm). Measure and cut the paper to this size. Using the bone folder, fold the paper into five valley folds (see figure 1). Be sure to leave a 1/2-inch (1.25 cm) tail at each end.

3 The middle ground concertina measures 4 x 24¾ inches (10 x 63 cm); measure, cut, and fold it you did in step 2.

4 The concertina that will hold the foreground prints measures 4 x 19¾ inches (10 x 50.25 cm); again, measure, cut, and fold it as you did in step 2.

5 Using the craft knife and the clear plastic ruler, measure and cut 1/8 inch (3 mm) from the edges of the background photos. Their final dimensions will be 3¾ x 5¾ inches (9.5 x 14.75 cm).

6 Using the bone folder, score each photo from the back, folding it exactly in half.

Materials

Strong yet flexible paper, such as card stock, cut to size as described below

4 x 6-inch (10 x 15.25 cm) photographs

Archival, double-sided adhesive tape

Waxed linen or other suitable thread

Tools

Clear plastic ruler

Craft knife

Bone folder

Awl or push pin

Tapestry or other blunt-ended needle

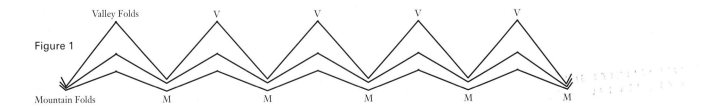

Valley Folds

Figure 1

Mountain Folds

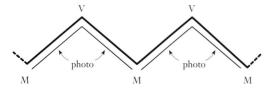

Figure 2

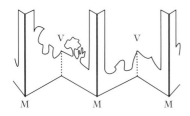

Figure 3

7 Using the double-sided adhesive tape, adhere each of the background images into the concertina with the deepest folds. Make sure the folds match exactly, and that ⅛-inch (.32 mm) of the paper is visible all around the edges of the print (see figure 2).

8 Measure and cut out the middle-ground photos. This print's final dimensions will be 3¾ x 4¾ inches (9.5 x 12 cm). Score and fold these as in step 6.

9 Use the double-sided adhesive to affix these prints to the middle ground concertina, as you did in step 7, making sure they line up exactly with the valley folds.

10 Using a craft knife, cut away various portions of the middle ground photographs (see figure 3). Be sure to leave the mountain folds unobstructed by the prints.

11 Measure and cut the foreground photos to their final dimensions of 3¾ x 3¾ inches (9.5 x 9.5 cm). Adhere these to the shallowest concertina with the double-sided adhesive tape. Cut away parts of these images, leaving only the interesting edges or large openings, so they can "frame" the photos behind it (see figure 4).

12 Nest the three concertinas into one another, and carefully mark three evenly spaced holes in all of the mountain folds.

13 Using the push pin or the awl, pierce the three holes.

14 With the waxed linen thread, sew the concertinas together at each mountain fold, using the three-hole pamphlet stitch. Following the diagram in figure 5, begin and end at the center hole. Finish by tying with a square knot (so it will lie flat) and cut the tails of the thread short.

15 When sewing at the tail ends of the nested concertinas, use an extra-long length of thread so you can knot it, then wrap it around the closed star. The wax will keep a simple knot from opening up.

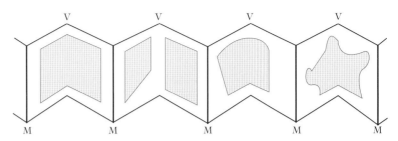

Figure 4

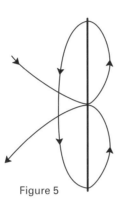

Figure 5

Sunday Best Stand-Up Figure

DESIGNER: **TERRY TAYLOR**

Somewhere in your albums is a perfectly adorable photograph of you, or someone you love, in their best grade-school finery. Don't keep it under wraps—show it off at the office or at the next birthday party. Who wouldn't love seeing a tender reminder of a more innocent age?

Materials

Photo (or copy of photo, enlarged to suit your purpose)

Foam-core board

Spray mount adhesive for photos

Tools

Metal-edge ruler

Pencil

Craft knife and replacement blades

Electric craft jigsaw with a fine-toothed blade (optional)

Hot glue gun and glue sticks

Instructions

1 Select your photo. If you do not wish to use an original photo, take the original to your local photo shop and have them make a copy. You can ask them to enlarge a specific part of the image and print it. This works well if you want to emphasize a particular person or thing in your selected photo.

2 Use a pencil to mark a piece of foam-core board that measures 8 x 10 inches (20 x 25 cm)—or larger or smaller, as your photo requires.

3 Work on a surface suitable for cutting, and use a metal-edge ruler as a guide to cut the foam-core board with the craft knife.

HINT: First make a shallow cut in the foam-core board, and then cut all the way through a second time, rather than trying to make a single, deep cut. The shallow cut will act as a guide that keeps your craft knife from slipping and ensures a straighter edge.

4 Follow the manufacturer's instructions for the spray mount adhesive you are using. Mount the photo on the foam-core board, smoothing it down from the center out to the edges with a clean, soft cloth.

5 You can cut the irregular outline of the foam-core figure by hand with a craft knife. It is tedious work to do, but it can be done. Better yet, use a small electric jigsaw (or any jigsaw with a fine blade) to cut out the silhouette of the figure.

6 To finish the stand-up figure, create an easel stand. Use a scrap of the foam-core board to create a triangle that measures about 6 inches (15 cm) on one straight side and $1^{1}/2$ inches (3.75 cm) on the other straight side. Cut out the triangle with a craft knife (use a metal-edge ruler to keep your cut clean and straight). Lean the cutout figure against the triangle's long side. To make the figure stand a bit better, use a craft knife (and metal-edge ruler) to angle the short side of the triangle; this helps the figure to lean back a bit.

7 Hold the triangle upright, the way it will stand when it is supporting the figure at the correct angle. With a hot glue gun, run a line of glue down the long side of the triangle, then quickly attach the figure to the triangular easel.

Materials

4 x 6-inch (10 x 15.25 cm) photographs

Archival, double-sided adhesive tape

Waxed linen thread (available at art supply stores)

5 pieces of stiff paper or cardstock, each 6¼ x 4¼ inches (16 x 12 cm)

2 pieces of stiff paper or cardstock, each 7½ x 4¼ inches (19 x 12 cm)

Glue stick

Tools

Craft knife

Clear plastic ruler

Awl or push pin

Tapestry or other blunt-ended needle

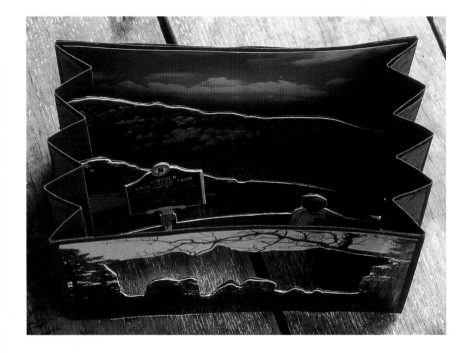

Instructions

Five photographs are cut and layered to reveal the ones that lie behind them, so keep this in mind as you're choosing the photographs. If you like, practice with cutouts of tracing-paper copies before using the actual prints; that way you can see if all the elements will work together the way you'd like them to.

1 Select five photographs, including background views, a main subject, and a framing image.

2 Using double-sided adhesive tape, adhere the prints to the five pieces of 6¼ x 4¼-inch (16 x 12 cm) paper.

3 Using a craft knife, cut away various portions of the photographs. For the foreground image leave only the interesting edges, so they can "frame" the rest of the pictures. The three middle photographs will be layered behind one another; each of these should have enough cut away to be able to reveal at least part of the background (see figure 1).

Figure 1

  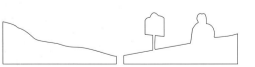 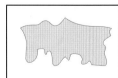

4 Construct two identical con-certinas from the 7 1/2 x 4 1/4-inch (19 x 12 cm) paper. Fold both of these with five valley folds (see figure 2).

5 Using the adhesive tape, attach one of the pieces of paper that measures 6 1/4 x 4 1/4 inches (19 x 12 cm) to one end of each of the concerti-nas. Mount the background photo-graph onto this back piece, but over the tail ends of the concertina, so that they are hidden (see figure 3).

6 In order to hide the tabs that hold the prints in place, they must be cut from the rear-facing side of the valley folds (see fig-ure 4). Set each of the photos in their respective folds to see where the tabs should be. Mark the con-certinas, then spread them flat. Use a small coin to trace a neat, half-round shape for the tabs, then cut along the mark with the craft knife.

7 Use the glue stick to attach the photos to the tabs.

8 Use the glue stick to attach the framing front image to the front end of the concertina (see figure 5).

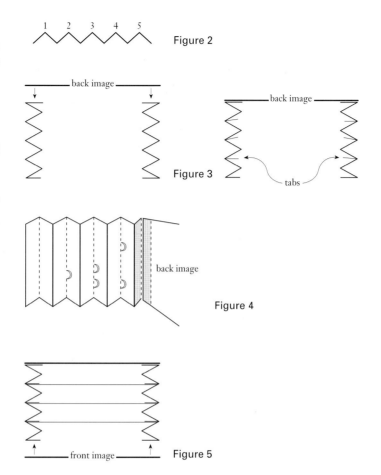

Figure 2

Figure 3

Figure 4

Figure 5

COLORING PRINTS
THE OLD-FASHIONED WAY

Materials for handcoloring, FROM TOP: Artist-grade colored pencils, photo oils, and photomarkers. *Photos by Tonya Evatt (left) and Suzanne Tourtillott (right)*

There is something so charming about the black-and-white photograph: it seems that it will always speak to us in a way that is distinctly different from the color print. This sense of a time and a place long past is beautifully emphasized with handcoloring, a technique as old as photography itself. Use color to highlight certain areas, or completely color the entire picture.

Photo oils, photomarkers, and artist-grade colored pencils are easy to find at large craft outlets and by mail order. Each method has unique qualities, letting the details in the image show through the color. Photo oils are best used on matte surface fiber base prints—they won't adhere to glossy ones at all without pretreating the surface with a matte spray. Colored pencils also require the "tooth" of a matte surface, and they can be used in combination with photo oils. The strokes used to apply them create interesting drawing effects and textures. Photomarkers, a new product on the market, combine the ease of pens with the transparency of oil and can be used on any sort of print surface. The Timeless Pastel Portrait, on page 43, shows how soft the color can be with this method.

The projects that follow demonstrate using photo oil paints and photo markers, the two most common techniques for handcoloring photographic prints. You're sure to be inspired when you see these examples, and you'll soon create your own intriguing works of art.

Harriet on the Beach
Handcolored Photo

DESIGNER: **DANA IRWIN**

Vintage family photographs—copied, enlarged, and colored—have a new vitality, and make wonderful conversation pieces. Photo oils, used on fiber base photo paper, can be either very intense or subtly muted; experimentation is simple to do. You can strengthen the color or add textured effects with artist-quality colored pencils, after the oils are completely dry.

Harriet Stryker and her friends   *Lake Superior — 1906*

Timeless Pastel Portrait

DESIGNER: **TONYA EVATT**

Soft, muted colors marry well with this charming subject. Even recent photographs can take on a timeless quality when they're spot-colored. With this simple approach, you can emphasize specific details, such as eye color or an unusual necktie, and minimize less-important areas.

Materials

Black-and-white photograph (either glossy or matte surface)

Distilled water

Measuring cup

Small bowl

Measuring spoons

Photo pre-wet solution (available where photography darkroom supplies are sold)

Clean sponge

Paper towels

Photo handcoloring marker pens

Tools

Blow dryer

Instructions

Be sure to work on a copy of the photo instead of the original. Use an enlargement that's at least 5 x 7 inches (12.75 x 17.75 cm), so the areas to be colored will be large enough.

1 Pour 8 ounces (240 mL) of distilled water into the small bowl and add a ¼ teaspoon (1.25 mL) of the pre-wet solution to it.

2 Dip the sponge into the pre-wet solution, squeezing excess solution from it so that the sponge is only moist.

3 Select the area of the print you wish to color first and moisten that area with the sponge. The print should be moist (tacky to the touch) and not wet. To avoid applying too much solution, blot the surface of the print with a paper towel.

4 Decide which colors will work best in which areas, using light colors for light areas, dark colors for darker areas. This assures even color distribution.

5 Using light circular motions, apply the color. Blot with a dry paper towel if the color puddles.

6 To remove color from any area, dip a corner of the sponge into the solution and lightly scrub the print.

7 When finished, dip and squeeze the entire sponge and wipe down the entire surface of the print once. Dry the print face up on a clean, dry surface, or use a blow dryer at the lowest speed setting, at a minimum of 12 inches (30.5 cm) from the print surface until it is no longer tacky or sticky.

CREATIVE PHOTOCOPYING

Think of the photocopier as a wonderful machine that not only makes duplicates of an original, but allows you to enlarge and reduce the size of a photograph, change its color, reverse the original and even print on acetate or fabric. It's a springboard for all sorts of imaginative uses of your photograph, and the operating instructions will be right there at the machine. The Elegant Lace Table on page 50 is an excellent example of creative photocopying.

The newest copy shops actually offer several services at one location, including photocopying, digital printing, and graphics—you can even get boards and papers cut for handmade books like Faye's Flip Books, on page 66.

"THE FORMULA FOR TAKING GREAT PHOTOGRAPHS IS TO THINK LIKE A POET."

IMOGEN CUNNINGHAM (1883–1976), WHO WAS STILL MAKING PICTURES INTO HER 90'S

THE PHOTOCOPIER IS A CREATIVE TOOL

The black-and-white photocopier transfers images onto paper or clear acetate by means of a powdery but durable toner. The color laser copier makes true-to-life color copies, but it can also completely change the color of your image with its color adjustment features. Some copiers have a sepia brown option that warms up the cool tones of black-and-white photographs.

Reduce or enlarge your image with the photocopier by entering the percentage of change in the size of the original. To calculate this percentage, divide the measurement of the width of the desired enlargement by the measurement of the width of the original size, then multiply the result by 100. To reduce, divide the width of the original by the width of the new size.

For example, a 4 x 6-inch print enlarged to 7 x 11 inches: $11 \div 6 = 1.833 \times 100$. The print should be enlarged by 183%. (Metric sizes are approximate: $28\,cm \div 17.75\,cm = 1.83$). To reduce an 8 x 10-inch print to 5 x 7 inches: $5 \div 8 = .625 \times 100$. The print should be reduced by 63%. (Metric sizes are approximate: $12.75\,cm \div 20.25\,cm = .629$).

Color Is Optional

If you're lucky enough to own a personal copier, you can buy different-colored toner cartridges to replace the standard black one—look at the Roman Pines Travel Book (page 57) to see how colored toner on colored paper creates an artistic look. Another option is to change the color of an original black-and-white print by color copying it. Color prints may not be able to capture the luminous colors you see on the computer monitor, but the Glowing Wedding Picture Lampshade on page 46 was made by altering the color copier's palette, which radically changed the appearance of the black-and-white photograph.

Transparencies on the Copier

Making acetate "negatives" is a snap with a black-and-white photocopier. Clear sheets of acetate are substituted for ordinary copier paper. Set up two or more snapshots on the copyglass to get the most out of each sheet of transparency material. These can then be used to make the blue fabric images for a Friends & Family Fabric Photo Album on page 66. Blueprinting doesn't require any kind of special equipment at all, and uses the sun to make the exposures.

COPYRIGHT CONSIDERATIONS

It's so easy to copy things nowadays, it might seem that the whole world of pictures is at your feet, ripe for the picking! But take a moment to remember that all creative works—images and words—are the property of their creator and are copyright-protected, whether they were taken by a portrait studio photographer or published in a magazine or book. Until the artist (or author, for that matter) has been dead for 75 years, he and his estate have the right to decide how and when those images are used, and even then copyrights may be renewed—so be sure to check it out. Obtain written permission before using or reproducing others' work, especially if you plan to sell it. Better yet, take the picture yourself, and gain the joy

This snapshot of Harry was photocopied onto acetate (overhead transparency) material for blueprinting

and satisfaction that comes from getting it just the way you want it.

Copyright laws are designed for your protection, too. Copyright your own work by putting the © symbol, your name, and the date on it. Then register it at the Register of Copyrights, Library of Congress, Washington DC 20559.

Both black-and-white and color photocopiers are the creative tools that let you transform your photographs into objects that will delight and amaze. You'll find yourself inspired to use the copier to help you decorate everything from lampshades to mirror frames in the next section.

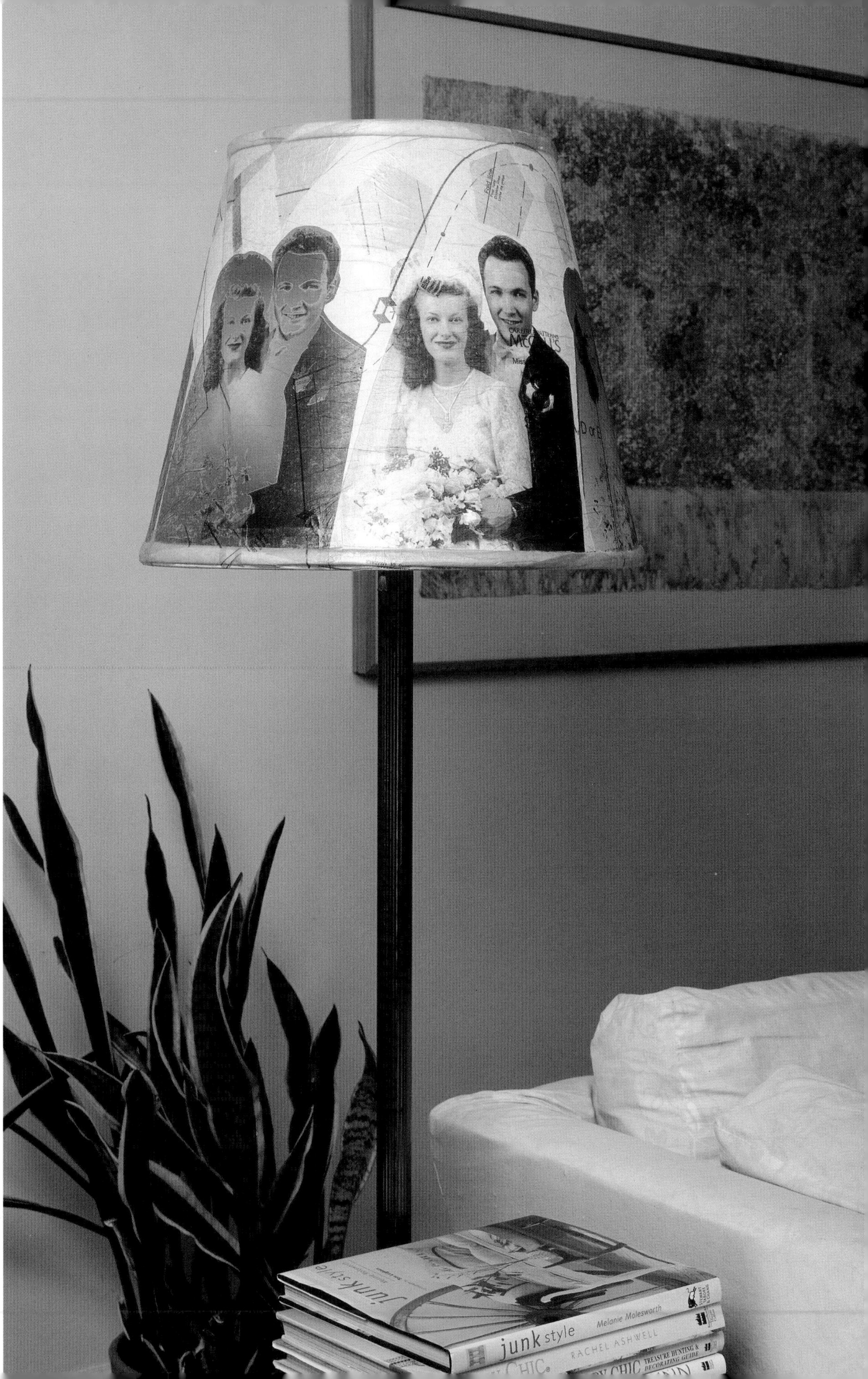
junk style
Melanie Molesworth
RACHEL ASHWELL

Glowing Wedding Picture Lampshade

DESIGNER: **ELLEN ZAHOREC**

Posterization was made popular by Andy Warhol's use of it in his famous images of Marilyn Monroe. An imaginative use of the color copier yielded a rainbow of images for this lampshade. The shade glows with warm memories of that special day.

Instructions

1 Measure the widest circumference of the shade with the tape measure. Determine how many trimmed prints are needed for your design. Since color copies are more expensive than ordinary photocopies, have plain black-and-white copies made to the size you wish. Use these to help you work out the design, proportion, and number of prints needed for the project.

2 Take an original print, if possible, to a copy shop that features the latest in color copiers. Ask the staff to make multiple copies, adjusting the color balance by means of the color palette on the copier. This will add unusual colors to the black-and-white image. Remember to have the original print enlarged during the color copying, if necessary.

3 Using scissors, cut away any unnecessary details from the color copies.

4 Following the manufacturer's directions, apply the spray adhesive to the back of one of the copies. Pick up the copy, turn it over, and hold it by the edges in a relaxed U shape, so the center of the paper will touch the shade first. Then carefully lower the sides down until the entire copy lies flat against the shade. This will minimize the appearance of bubbles and wrinkles.

5 Supporting the shade from the inside with your hand, gently smooth down the copy from the center out to the edges.

6 With the wide brush, apply the découpage sealer over the photocopies.

7 Before the découpage has dried, lay old dress patterns on the shade. Brush on another layer of sealer; let it dry.

8 Trim any excess from the edges with a craft knife.

Materials

A selection of posterized color copier prints from a black-and-white photo

Spray adhesive

Découpage medium

Stiff paper lampshade

Tools

Tape measure

Scissors

Craft knife

Wide, square paintbrush

Transparent Transfer Ornaments

DESIGNER: **LYNN B. KRUCKE**

Favorite snapshots become personalized decorations that will be enjoyed from year to year. They also make memorable gifts... just tailor the photograph to suit the occasion.

Materials

Adhesive-backed clear laminating sheet (NOT the heat-seal type)

Photograph

Pencil

Water

Clear glass ornament (with removable cap)

Ribbon for embellishment

Tools

Ruler

Scissors

Compass or circle cutter

Tweezers

Instructions

Light areas on a photograph will be very sheer once they're transferred, so images with more color and contrast will give better results than, say, a snow scene.

1 Make a color copy of the photograph.

2 Using a ruler, measure the diameter of the ornament.

3 With the compass or the circle cutter, pencil, and scissors, cut out a circle from the clear laminating sheet. The diameter of the circle should be slightly (approximately ⅛ inch or 3 mm) smaller than the diameter of the ornament. To determine its diameter, place the sphere on a sheet of paper. Hold two flat sticks against opposing sides of the sphere, and mark where they touch the paper; then measure the marks with a ruler.

4 Remove the paper backing from the laminating sheet. Centering the clear sheet over the color copy (not the original photograph!), carefully adhere the two together.

5 Smooth out the laminating sheet to remove any air bubbles. Trim excess paper with scissors.

6 Submerge the laminated image in water for at least 15 minutes. Once the paper is thoroughly saturated, begin rubbing the color copy away from the back of the laminating sheet. The toner will have transferred to the clear laminating sheet. Be patient and rub away as much of the paper fiber as possible. Sometimes it's hard to tell if you've gotten it all until the piece dries. If necessary, rewet and rub some more.

7 Once dry, trim the top of the circle slightly into more of an oval shape.

8 Remove the cap from the ornament. Carefully roll the transfer into a tight cylinder, and slip this into the ornament. Once inside, it will uncurl to fill the ornament. Use tweezers to adjust the placement of the transfer.

9 Replace the cap onto the ornament, and embellish as desired with ribbon.

Faye's Flip Books

DESIGNER: **DANA IRWIN**

In the tiny world of flip books, a little girl can go from roller-skater to glamour-puss in seconds flat, or do a happy dance in a meadow. It may look high-tech, but all it really takes is a little bit of forethought, and an enthusiastic model.

Materials

Photocopies of black-and-white contact sheets

Colored card stock or heavy-weight paper, cut to fit the size of the contact sheet frames

Rubber stamps, markers, or other decorative items

Tools

Scissors

Instructions

1 Plan your photo "story." Sketch it out, if it will help you visualize what you want to illustrate.

2 Looking through the camera's viewfinder, map out the "stage" (with rocks, sticks, or whatever you like) where the subject will be "performing." Keep the action area to the right side of the frame, to allow room for the book's binding at the left side.

3 With the camera on a tripod or set on a flat, sturdy surface (such as a chair or a wall), shoot each frame with the subject moving very slowly, if possible. In order to achieve a realistic impression of movement, shoot the entire session from the same vantage point; don't move the camera at all.

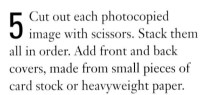

4 Have contact sheets made. Photocopy three or four copies of each contact sheet, enlarged to 200 to 400 percent.

5 Cut out each photocopied image with scissors. Stack them all in order. Add front and back covers, made from small pieces of card stock or heavyweight paper.

6 In the phone book, find a quick printer that handles small jobs. Have them glue the edges into a tablet-style binding, and also trim the three open sides of the book, so they have straight edges. Ask them to glue a binding cover on.

7 Embellish the covers with rubber stamps or other decorative techniques.

Heartfelt PhotoCollage Card

DESIGNER: **KATHY ANDERSON**

Celebrate someone who is near and dear with a collage card that combines both modern and nostalgic elements. A color copy of a vintage photo is accompanied by coordinating papers and creative rubberstamping techniques and materials. The decorative theme continues on the inside of the card and on the envelope.

Instructions

1 Roll the streamer-pattern brayer over the colorless stamp pad and roll one pass over the dark red paper. Sprinkle the clear embossing powder over the paper, tap off the excess, and melt the embossing powder with the heat gun.

2 Tear the gold metallic paper in about half at a pleasing angle.

3 Roll the mesh-pattern brayer over the permanent black stamp-pad ink, then roll it over one of the gold metallic paper pieces. Let dry.

4 Tear the dark green paper into a 1-inch (2.5 cm) strip, and tear the tissue paper to a slightly larger size than that of your photocopied image.

5 Glue down the dark red paper first, covering the entire front of the card. Glue the metallic gold paper on the right front side of the card over the red paper. Glue the tissue paper to the left side of the card, then position and glue the color copy of your photo on top of that. Glue the dark green strip of paper at the right edge of the photocopy, overlapping it slightly.

6 Using the permanent black stamp pad, apply the greeting stamp to the lower right corner of the metallic gold paper. Apply the foil corner in the upper right corner, and the cancelled stamp just above the greeting stamp.

7 Tie the metallic threads to the heart charm, and glue the heart onto the dark green paper.

8 With a dry craft paintbrush, or your fingertip, rub a small amount of each of the two colored embossing powders onto the torn edge of the photocopied picture.

9 If any of the papers extend beyond the outside dimension of the card, trim off those edges with a sharp craft knife and a metal straightedge.

10 Tear a 3-inch (7.5 cm) square piece of scrap paper for masking off the message area on the inside of the card. Position it on the right side. Roll the patterned brayer onto the clear stamp pad, then roll it across the entire inside of the card. Remove the scrap of paper.

11 Sprinkle the metallic gold embossing powder over the clear pattern that was rolled inside the card. Tap off the excess, and set the powder with a heat gun.

12 Tear two pieces of paper, placing them in the envelope-address and return-address areas; repeat the embossing procedure from steps 10 and 11.

13 Arrange scraps of metallic gold, red, and green papers around the area left for the message; glue them down.

14 Use your finger to coil the 1/8-inch-wide (3 mm) strip of copper, then flatten the coil with a heavy book. Glue it in place inside the card.

Materials

Clear pigment (colorless) stamp pad

Embossing powders, 1 clear (colorless), 1 metallic gold, 1 metallic copper, and 1 pearlescent

Handmade papers, each about 7 inches (17.75 cm) square, in dark red, dark green, metallic, and Japanese tissue

Black permanent ink stamp pad

White glue

5 x 7-inch (12.75 x 17.75 cm) greeting card and matching envelope

Rubber stamp greeting

Decorative foil corner

Cancelled postage stamp

Metallic threads

Heart charm

Color photocopy of your favorite photo (use a sepia color for a vintage look) to approximately 2 1/2 inches (6.25 cm) square

One 6 x 1/8-inch (15.25 x 3 mm) strip of lightweight copper sheet

Tools

Textured rubber stamp brayers, 1 mesh pattern and 1 streamer pattern

Heat gun or blow dryer for embossing

Greeting stamp ("Thank You" was used here)

Metal-edged ruler

Craft knife

Materials

School photos

White or cream card stock

Clip frame 9 x 12-inch
(22.75 x 30.5 cm)

Sheet of white paper the same
size as the frame

Glue or rubber cement

Colored markers

Tools

Scissors

Craft knife

School Friends Frame

DESIGNER: **CONNIE MATRICARDI**

Here's a wonderful opportunity for you to work with your child on a colorful project that you'll both enjoy for years to come. The frame can hold a photo or a special piece of artwork, or you might make photocopies of the finished piece that can be given as gifts to the classmates whose pictures were used as the frame's motif.

Instructions

1 Photocopy the school photos on a black-and-white photocopier, enlarging or reducing them as necessary so your copies are close to 1¾ x 2¼ inches (3.5 cm x 5.7 cm) in size. Lighten or darken them, if necessary. Use the "photo" option if the copier has one—it will make a much better copy.

2 Cut out each photo to the same size. Trim if necessary. You will need 16 photocopies, so either use 16 different photos, copy fewer photos several times, or just duplicate one photo and use it alone.

3 Arrange the photos around the perimeter of the sheet of paper, starting at the corners. Make sure the photos are evenly spaced and flush with the edges of the paper. Glue each photo onto the paper.

4 Using markers, color the photo frame. Add other embellishments, such as paint and glitter, as desired.

5 You can place a small drawing or photo in the center of the finished frame, or cut out a window in the center, and use it as a mat. Assemble the clip frame and hang.

Roman Pines Travel Book

DESIGNER: **EVELYN ELLER**

Photo highlights of a trip to Rome are featured in this distinctive memory book. Warm-toned photocopies of snapshots, plus text and maps from local guidebooks, were imaginatively combined on pages of different sizes. You might use prose or poetry of your own composition printed onto a medium-weight handmade rice paper.

Materials

Green acrylic iridescent paint

Butcher or other large white paper to use as scrap

Waxed paper

Linen thread

Acid-free adhesive in a jar, or glue stick

Text paper: 2 full 22 x 30-inch (56 x 76 cm) sheets of cream-colored heavy-weight, acid-free paper with a deckle edge; and 1 tan-colored sheet of the same type, cut to size as described below

Cover paper: 1 full sheet tan-colored heavy-weight paper, cut to size as described below

Medium-weight tan and cream handmade and rice papers, cut to a standard sheet size, or tinted and textured papers of the correct size and weight for use in a photocopier (see Creative Photocopying, page 44).

Tools

Acrylic cutting board, reserved for craft use only

Hake or other broad-bristled brush

Small plastic nonfood container

Iron

Scissors

Craft knife

Metal ruler

Bone folder

Pencil

Push pins or awl

Tapestry needle or blunt-ended needle with a large eye

Number 2 acrylic paintbrush

Instructions

1 Dilute about one-third of the green acrylic iridescent paint with 2 ounces (60 mL) of water in the plastic container. Thoroughly mix them together with the hake brush.

2 Put a sheet of the cream-colored handmade paper on the acrylic cutting board. Using the hake brush, paint the entire surface of the paper beginning from the center and working out to the edges in all directions. To keep fingerprints off the painted side, slip your fingers under the edges and move the paper to a large sheet of butcher or other white paper until dry.

3 Put the entire painted sheet inside a folded sheet of clean white paper. Flatten the painted paper on a hard surface, using an iron set at a low temperature.

4 Photocopy the photographs, maps, and text onto the assorted handmade, rice, and green-painted papers, or use a selection of assorted tinted and textured papers suitable for running through a photocopier. Cut the images, if necessary, to sizes that will fit on the larger pages.

5 Measure and cut one 12 x 22-inch (30.5 x 56 cm) piece from the tan acid-free paper, making sure the deckle edges are along the long side.

6 Lay a piece of waxed paper over the fold area to protect it. Fold the paper in half with the bone folder, to a finished size of 12 x 11 inches (30.5 x 28 cm).

7 Measure and cut two 7½ x 22-inch (19 x 56 cm) pieces from the cream paper, deckle edges on the long side. Fold in half, to a finished size of 7½ x 11 inches (19 x 28 cm).

8 Measure and cut one 12½ x 23½-inch (31.75 x 60 cm) piece from the tan acid-free paper, for the cover; the finished size of the book will be 11½ x 12½ inches (29.25 x 31.75 cm). Fold the cover sheet in half, as you did in step 7. The cover will overlap the pages by a ½ inch (1.25 cm).

9 Slip the papers, one inside the other, starting with the 12 x 11-inch tan paper for the cover. Then, alternate stacking the cream and tan heavyweight papers on top of one another, centering each one over the others.

10 Measure five evenly spaced holes along the spine, marking them with a pencil. Use an awl or push pins to make the holes.

11 Sew the paper together with the linen thread, using a simple in-and-out running stich (sometimes called a pamphlet stitch). Begin on the outside at the center hole, making sure the last stitch comes out at the center hole (see figure 1). Finish by braiding these tail threads together.

12 Position the photos and text on all the pages. Apply glue only to the edges of the backs of the photocopies. Cover the glued areas with waxed paper, then smooth them with the edge of the bone folder.

13 Put the book under a heavy weight until completely dry.

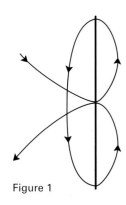

Figure 1

Vacation Mirror Mat & Frame

DESIGNER: **ELLEN ZAHOREC**

In this imaginative project, photographic images don't just sit in a frame—they are the decorative motif of the frame itself. Even if the original photographs are color, using a standard photocopier will convert them all into tones of cool grays, black, and white.

Materials

Frame/mat/glass package

Color and black-and-white photocopies

Adhesive spray mount

Acrylic spray sealer or découpage medium

Tools

Scissors with decorative edges

Instructions

1 Take your favorite old photos from past family trips—the ones still sitting in the messy box in the closet—and make black-and-white copies at a photocopy shop. To make the most of your money, arrange your photos face down on the copy glass within the marks that indicate the largest-size paper available. For better-quality copies of photographs, use the "photo" option on the copier. Have several of these large copies made.

2 Buy an inexpensive frame package with mat and glass at a local craft shop. Disassemble it.

3 Cut your photocopies apart, using decorative-edge scissors for greater visual interest.

4 Following the manufacturer's instructions, use the adhesive spray for mounting. Be sure to use it in a ventilated area, spraying only a few at a time. To begin, center an important image on the upper frame section. Working out from here, cover the frame with the cutout copied images, folding them carefully around to the back side. Firmly smooth them down to eliminate any wrinkles. Allow the adhesive to dry.

5 Use an acrylic spray or découpage medium to seal and protect the surface. Let it dry, then reassemble the frame package.

Heat-transfer sheets and photo transfer medium are two popular ways to put photographic images onto fabric.

FROM IMAGE TO FABRIC AND MORE

There are a lot of ways to transfer photocopied images onto other materials. Nearly all the transfer projects in this book are versatile enough that you have the option of which transfer method to use, though the appearance of the image varies somewhat in each process. Compare an image transferred onto paper using acetone, such as the *Memento Mori* Cards on page 76, to those on the Eco-Friendly Photo-Tote, on page 69.

CHEMICAL AGENTS

Solvent transfers—in the form of various liquids and pastes—are inexpensive and simple to do. While their methods of application vary, for most solvents you simply make a photocopy of your print, coat the photocopy with the chemical agent, place the coated photocopy on the fabric, and use a brayer or even an old spoon to rub the image onto the fabric. You'll need to heat-set the image by ironing on the reverse side after the transfer is completely dry.

Photo transfer medium, acetone, liquid solvent, and paint stripper are all effective solvents, and all are used for projects in this book, from the clever Carmen Miranda Doll on page 64 to the Gracious Girls Pillow on page 72.

PHOTO TRANSFER SHEETS

These versatile sheets of specially treated paper are widely used, partly because they can produce a high-quality transfer. Using them is a two-step process. First you must get the image onto the transfer sheet; then, the image from the transfer sheet is moved onto the fabric.

The most common means of getting an image onto the transfer sheet is via the photocopier; the coated sheets fit nicely into the paper drawer. Alternatively, if you've gone digital—if you have a computer, a printer, and a means of importing digitized images into your computer—you can print your images directly onto the transfer sheets. Many printer and photocopier manufacturers make transfer sheets specifically for their equipment, so buy accordingly, and be sure to read and follow their instructions. (A thrifty tip: try to get as many images as possible onto the transfer paper, then cut them apart for later use.)

Once the image is on the transfer sheet, it is then transferred to the fabric by heat—you iron it on. Most full-service copy shops will do either or both of these steps for you. That is, you can take in your print and have it transferred to a photo transfer sheet; some will even transfer the image onto whatever fabric you supply.

While solvents and transfer sheets are the most common methods, you'll find other options to play with. For example, you can have a rubber stamp made from your favorite photo and then do with it what you will (see the RubberSoul Portrait Shirt on page 78 and the Too Cool for School Card Portrait Card on page 80). There's even an ingenious "blueprint" fabric that receives an image when it's exposed to the sun; see the Friends & Family Fabric Photo Album on page 66.

IMAGE REVERSAL

Note that most transfer methods reverse the image (and any words!) onto the fabric, so if you don't want this to happen, make a "mirror image" photocopy before transferring it onto either the transfer sheet or the fabric.

Whatever method you choose, the effects of photographic image transfer can be modern or nostalgic, depending on the subject matter and how you decide to handle it. The projects that follow are inspired examples that range from the purely practical to the highly decorative, from fabric to paper and beyond.

Carmen Miranda Doll

DESIGNER:
JEAN TOMASO MOORE

Transform a lighthearted image into an heirloom-worthy keepsake by using personal mementos, such as jewelry and fabric scraps, to add character and unique style to your creation.

Instructions

1 Using a color photocopier, enlarge or reduce your photo to approximately 11 x 17 inches (28 x 43 cm). Be sure to use the mirror-image option, so the image will be facing the right way after it's transferred to the fabric.

2 Carefully cut away any extraneous background from the image on the color copy. Cut a square of muslin slightly larger than the copied image.

3 Using a foam brush or large paintbrush, coat the entire copy of the image with photo transfer medium. Be sure to read and follow the manufacturer's directions before beginning this process.

4 Place the coated image face down onto the muslin. Press down firmly with your hands, smoothing away any air pockets with your fingers. Use the brayer to ensure even pressure, rolling it across the image in all directions. Clean up any excess medium that seeps out around the edges with a damp cloth. Allow the image to dry with the photocopy in place for 24 hours.

5 Soak the fabric in water for 10 minutes. Remove and carefully rub the paper away from the fabric to reveal the image underneath. The photocopy is now transferred to the fabric. Once again, allow it to dry. Then, trim all the excess fabric away from the image.

6 Using acrylic paints and a brush, add color to the two pieces of plain muslin fabric. Allow the painted muslin to dry, then iron each unpainted side to remove wrinkles.

7 Lay out a piece of the painted muslin, face up. Using fabric glue, adhere the cutout photo transfer figure to the painted muslin. Using the brayer, press and smooth out any air bubbles.

8 To add visual interest and depth to the image, arrange an assortment of silk flowers on the fabric and affix them with white craft glue. You can also add a tiny piece of tulle or netting fabric to the hair where a bow, hat, or head piece would sit. Attach it with white craft glue.

9 Lay the second piece of painted muslin face down. Lay the transfer, which is now glued to a piece of painted muslin, on top of the face down piece.

10 Using a sewing machine or sewing by hand, sew around the entire image, through both layers of the painted muslin, but leave a small border around the figure. Also leave a small opening near the bottom. Cut away all the excess painted muslin, leaving $1/2$-inch (1.25 cm) border next to the stitch line.

11 Loosely stuff polyester fiberfill through the opening you left at the bottom. Use a pencil to push the fiberfill into tight spots. Do not overstuff. Sew the opening closed by hand.

12 Finish the doll by embellishing with antique buttons, rhinestones, and bits of old jewelry and fabric trim.

Materials

Full-length photograph of a person

3 pieces of muslin fabric, 15 x 20 inches (38 x 51 cm)

Photo transfer medium

Acrylic paint (blue, green, and black were used here)

Silk flowers and berries for bottom of dress

Small scrap of fabric tulle/netting

Polyester fiberfill

Old jewelry, fabric scraps, rhinestones, baubles

Tools

Scissors

Foam brush or large paintbrush

Acrylic brayer or rolling pin

Damp cloth

Iron

Fabric glue

White craft glue

Sewing machine or needle and thread

Pencil

Friends & Family Fabric Photo Album

DESIGNER: **LOIS SIMBACH**

The design on each page of this fabric album centers around the unusual blue-printed pictures made from snapshots. From there, your imagination can go romantic, comedic, or nostalgic, to reflect your subject's personality. Any page can be the "cover"—when the mood strikes, you need only flip to that particular page for a new look. Keep it complete as a book, adding new pages as the mood strikes you, framc individual pages and give them as gifts, or assemble them together as a wall hanging!

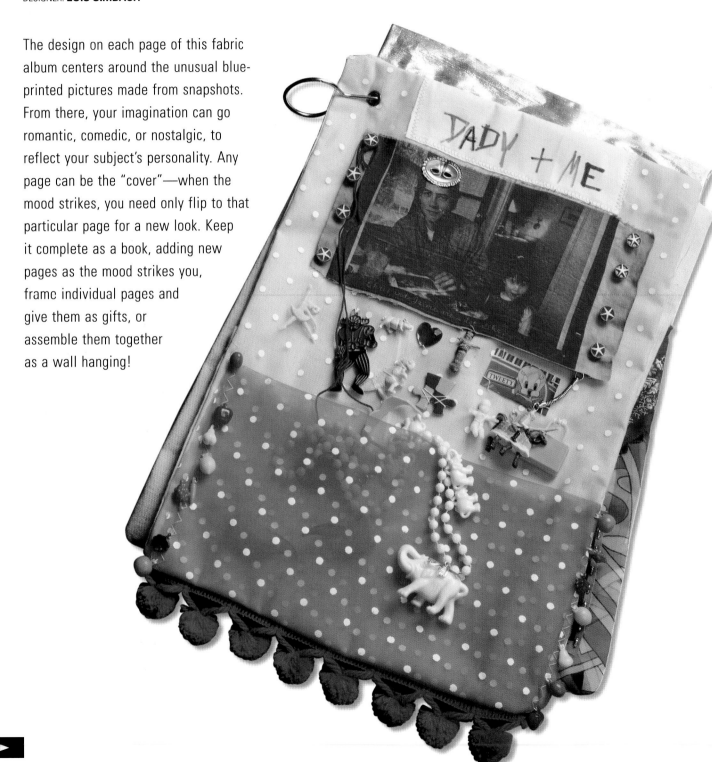

Instructions

Take the time to plan the design. Sketch your design ideas on a piece of paper, or assemble the actual elements you'll be using and experiment with different placements, starting with the larger elements. The muslin backing and pocket on each page add stability, give it a finished look, and provide a place to put more photos or items you plan to add in the future. The fun blueprint material lets you use the sun to transfer photo images to fabric.

1 With a fabric-marking tool, measure and mark the canvas for the final dimension, adding $1\frac{1}{4}$ inches (3 cm) in each direction. This provides a $\frac{5}{8}$-inch (1.5 cm) seam allowance.

2 Using scissors, cut along your marks. Cut two pieces of material (front and back) for each "page."

3 On the right sides of the material, mark the position for the grommet (or buttonhole) at a point that is $2\frac{5}{8}$ inches (6.75 cm) in from the top left edge and $2\frac{5}{8}$ inches (6.75 cm) in from the left side.

4 Away from direct sunlight, remove a single piece of the pretreated blueprint cotton fabric. Laying the fabric on the corrugated cardboard, staple the fabric to the cardboard using an opened stapler.

5 Lay the acetate negative, centered and right side up, on the fabric. There should be a small amount of extra fabric around all the edges. Lay a sheet of clean, double-strength window glass on top of this.

6 Put this stack in direct sunlight, or very close to a sunny window, for several minutes. The time can vary due to several variables, so consult the manufacturer's directions for guidelines.

7 When the fabric has been adequately exposed, carry the exposed blueprint materials away from the sunlight. Remove the fabric from the cardboard by using a small screwdriver to pull out the staples.

8 Immediately immerse the exposed fabric in a dishtub partially filled with cool water. Flush the chemicals from the fabric by running water into the tub for several minutes, until the water stays clear. Hang the blueprint to dry, out of direct sunlight.

9 Press all the fabric pieces flat with a steam iron on the ironing board. To protect the blueprints, lay them face down within a folded piece of plain cotton fabric before pressing them.

10 With a sharp pair of scissors, trim the blueprint to the desired size.

11 Stitch the blueprint to the front canvas piece; here, a zigzag stitch was made with a sewing machine.

Materials

Cotton canvas

Presensitized blueprint fabric

Acetate negatives (see Transparencies on the Copier, page 45)

Plain piece of cotton fabric for ironing

Corrugated cardboard

Trim, buttons, trinkets, and charms as needed

Fabric paint or pigment ink as needed

Metal shower curtain ring

Pretreated blueprint fabric*

Tools

Fabric-marking tool

Tape measure

Scissors

Stapler and staples

8 x 10-inch (20.25 x 25.5 cm) sheet of double-strength glass, edges covered with masking tape for safe handling

Small screwdriver

Dishtub

Steam iron and ironing board

Sewing machine (optional)

Needle

Sewing thread

Grommet-setting tool, or sewing machine with buttonhole feature

Decorative painting tools, such as paintbrushes, sponge stencils, and rubber stamps

* Blueprint fabric may be ordered from:

Blueprints-Printables
1504 #7 Industrial Way
Belmont CA 94002

(800) 356-0445

12 Add other decorative elements as desired, using your sketch as a guide. Some suitable techniques are sponged stencil designs, machine or hand embroidery, beading and appliqué, and pigment ink with rubber stamps. Painting may be done before or after sewing the front and back together, but decorative sewing and most attachments—staples, rivets, and the like—should be done first, so their undersides will be hidden in the finished piece. If you are using decorative trim (such as piping, lace, or pompoms) at the edges, pin it on top of the seam allowance before sewing the front and back pieces together.

13 With right sides together, stitch around the sides of the fabric page pieces along the seam allowance. Leave part of the last side open.

14 Closely trim off the excess seam allowance at the corners. This reduces the bulk of the material after it is turned right-side out.

15 Press the seams open.

16 Turn the material right side out. Use a pin to pull out the corners more fully. Turn in the seam allowance at the opening to make a neat closure, then press the edges flat through the back (plain) side of the "page." Keep the iron away from decorative trim or protect it with plain cotton cloth.

17 Whipstitch the opening closed with needle and thread.

18 Attach the grommet, or make a buttonhole, at the mark in the upper left corner that was made earlier.

19 Continue to add decorative paint elements, as desired. When all the "pages" are finished, thread them onto the shower curtain ring.

Eco-Friendly PhotoTote

DESIGNER: **LOIS SIMBACH**

Whether you're doing a bit of shopping or returning library books, don't resort to plastic grocery bags; instead, personalize a plain canvas tote with a one-of-a-kind photo. You can promote your own business, or just enjoy the unique look of this perfectly practical, reusable carryall.

Materials

Photocopy of a photograph

Heat transfer sheet

Cotton fabric, cut to fit front of tote

Thread

Plain canvas tote bag

Tools

Scissors

Iron

Sewing machine with zigzag stitch option

Instructions

1 Transfer the photograph to the heat-transfer sheet with a photocopier. To take advantage of the full size of the transfer material, arrange as many pictures as possible on the transfer paper. Leave a bit of space around each one for easy trimming.

2 Carefully cut out the transfer with sharp scissors.

3 Lay out the piece of cotton fabric, right side up, on a hard, smooth surface. Transfer the image to the fabric with a very hot iron, using your weight to apply as much pressure as possible.

4 While it's still warm, peel off the backing paper. Trim the photo transfer with a sharp pair of scissors to the desired size.

5 Use the sewing machine to zigzag-stitch the photo transfer to the front of the tote.

Fond Memories
Felt Pin   DESIGNER: **BETTY AUTH**

A "heart-felt" pin, embellished with beads and trinkets, carries the memory
of someone near and dear. Felt is a fun and easy material to work with.

Instructions

1 Using tracing paper and a pencil, trace two hearts from the pattern onto the pieces of mat board, and cut them out with the craft knife.

2 Round off the corners of the 5-inch-square (12.5 cm) piece of felt.

3 Size your photo to fit within the boundaries of the heart pattern, then print it onto the transfer sheet. Iron the transfer onto the cream or white felt. Trim the edges of the transferred image and set it aside.

4 With the sewing needle and beading thread, hand-sew a line of ¼-inch-long (6 mm) gathering stitches around the edges of the 5-inch (12.5 cm) square piece of felt. Pull up slightly, and insert a small handful of fiberfill.

5 Lay one of the mat-board hearts inside the pouch that you've created out of felt and fiberfill. Pull up the gathers, and add more fiberfill as needed to make a puffy heart. Tighten the gathers at the back of the heart. Take a few stitches across the back in several directions, joining the sides of the gathered felt. Secure with a knot and tie off. Trim the thread.

6 Smear a little glue on the back of the trimmed felt photo, and position the photo on the front of the heart. Allow it to dry.

7 With the embroidery needle and pearl cotton thread, use a blanket stitch or other decorative stitch to tack down the edges of the photo. Keep the stitches small and near the edges.

8 Decorate the heart with embroidery stitches, beads, and fringe as desired.

9 Glue the second mat heart to the back of the pin, covering all the raw edges. Weight the pin down by placing a book on top of it until the glue is dry.

10 Glue the back of the pin high on the back of the heart. Let it dry.

Materials
FOR 1 UNFRINGED HEART

Tracing paper

2 pieces mat board, each at least 3½ inches (8.8 cm) square

5-inch (12.5 cm) square of felt in a color of your choice

3-inch (7.5 cm) square white or cream felt

Iron-on photographic transfer sheet

Small black-and-white photograph

#5 pearl cotton embroidery thread in colors to coordinate with felt

Beading thread

Polyester fiberfill

Beads and charms for embellishment

Jewelry pin back

Tools

Pencil

Craft knife

Scissors

Iron

Regular sewing needle

White craft glue

Sharp embroidery needle with large eye, or crewel embroidery needle

Gracious Girls Pillow

DESIGNER: **PAT SCHEIBLE**

These lovely girls are captured on an embellished pillow that glows with good manners. Scour your photo albums for charming images, and surprise family members with warm, personal mementos at holiday time.

Instructions

The transfer method you use is optional, but be aware that most methods will reverse the image, so make your photocopy with the mirror-image option if you want the photograph to remain in its original orientation.

1 Tape the fabric to the glass, pulling it taut.

2 Lay the photocopy face down on the fabric, and tape it all the way around at the edges.

3 Wearing the rubber gloves, drop about 1 teaspoon of paint stripper onto the photocopy and rub it in well, applying pressure with the back of the spoon. The solvent in the stripper softens the photocopy toner, which is then transferred onto the fabric by the pressure of the spoon. You can lift a corner from time to time to see how the transfer is progressing.

4 Remove the photocopy paper when the image has transferred completely to the fabric. Hand wash in gentle soap to remove any traces of stripper and let dry.

5 Using a low temperature setting, iron the back side of the transfer.

6 Color the image, if you wish, using fabric paints, according to the manufacturer's instructions.

7 Using the shank-type buttons, attach the finished doily to a pillow. Embellish with tiny knots or bows of ribbon.

Materials

Photocopy of your photograph

Solvent-based semipaste paint stripper

Linen doily

Fabric paints, optional

Mild dishsoap

Vintage shank-type buttons

1/8-yard (15 cm) ribbon

Pillow

Tools

Sheet of glass

Masking tape

Rubber gloves

Old spoon

Iron

Small craft paintbrush, optional

Needle and coordinating thread

Memories of Granny Pillow

DESIGNER: **NANCY WORRELL**

Materials

Photocopy of photograph

Photocopy transfer medium or heat-transfer sheet

¼ yard (20 x 20 cm) of unbleached muslin

Small, round crocheted doily, approximately 5 inches (12.75 cm) in diameter

Antique or tea-dyed handkerchief, approximately 10 inches (25 cm) square

Variety of white buttons

Coordinating thread

Polyester fiberfill

Tools

Scissors

Iron

Pins

Needle or sewing machine

Measuring tape

Remember Granny every day with this dainty, antique-handkerchief pillow. This is an excellent way to incorporate your heirloom linens into your everyday life. If you don't have any heirloom linens, check out estate and garage sales, or purchase doilies at your local craft store and antique them using a dye made of strong, brewed black tea.

Instructions

1 Tear the photocopied image from the paper. Cut a square of muslin approximatcly 1 inch (2.5 cm) larger than the photocopied image. Follow the manufacturer's directions (using either photo transfer medium or a heat-transfer sheet), transfer the photocopy to the muslin. After the transfer is complete, trim the excess fabric to the edge of the transferred photo.

2 To assemble the pillow top, center the doily on the handkerchief and pin it into place. Center the transfer on the doily. Arrange the buttons to make a pleasing frame around the image. Tack the buttons in place, stitching the doily to the handkerchief at the same time.

3 For this pillow, the handkerchief border becomes a flange. Measure across the center of the handkerchief from border to border. To these measurements add a ⅝-inch (1.5 cm) seam allowance, and cut two muslin squares. Use a sewing machine or hand-stitch the squares together, leaving an opening for turning. Carefully trim the corners, and turn the squares right sides out; stuff with fiberfill. Blind-stitch the opening closed with a needle and thread.

4 To finish the pillow, center the handkerchief top on the pillow. Using the needle and coordinating thread, whip or blind-stitch the pillow top to the muslin pillow form.

Memento Mori Cards

DESIGNER: **NICOLE TUGGLE**

Loosely translated from the Latin, *memento mori* means "to the memory of one who is gone." Here, a vacation snapshot of an ancient sculptured bust is the inspiration for several lovely variations of embellished greeting cards.

Materials

Blank card

Photocopy of photograph (fresh copies work best)

Masking tape

Handmade paper (any texture, any color)

Liquid solvent

Craft glue

Seed beads

Thin thread or fishing line

Assorted paper scraps or mementos for embellishment (optional)

Tools

Paintbrush

Burnishing tool (dull butter knife or the back of a spoon)

Scissors

Sewing needle or awl

Beading needle

Instructions

Because the addition of embellishments may increase the weight of the card, you may need to add extra postage. Depending on the texture of the paper used for your final piece, the image may be slightly distorted. Experiment with different textures for the desired results.

1 Photocopy one or more photographs.

2 Place the image side of the selected photocopy down onto the paper. Hold it firmly, or tape it down on all sides with masking tape.

3 Spread the solvent evenly over the photocopy, covering the entire image. Use a dull butter knife or bone folder to burnish the photocopy. This helps transfer the image onto the surface of the paper.

4 Carefully lift up the photocopy and discard. You should now have a mirror image of your original picture.

5 Cut the transferred image to the desired size and glue it onto the front of the blank card.

6 To embellish with seed beads, use a running (pamphlet) stitch through the card front along the sides of the image, adding beads as you go. If you are using stiff card stock, you may first need to poke holes through the card, using a regular sewing needle or awl, before using the beading needle.

7 For additional embellishment, glue on paper scraps, small mementos, or scraps of metal. Whatever materials you use, make sure you can still slip the finished card into the envelope.

RubberSoul Portrait Shirt

DESIGNER: **TERRY TAYLOR**

Materials

Cotton T-shirt

Rubberstamp made from
   a photograph

Stamp pad inked with
   fabric ink

Scrap of cardboard about
   8 x 10 inches (20.25 x 25 cm)

2 colors of acrylic paint

Tools

2 corks of different sizes

Jar lid, or similar container,
   for paint

Iron

NOTE: Providing a photograph that's
camera-ready will save you some
money. If you have a computer,
scanner, and graphics program at
home, you can scan the photograph
as line art (not grayscale), make it
the correct size for the stamp, and
then print out the photo. Bring this
to the rubber stamp company.

In the earliest days of photography, some superstitious folks thought
that the camera could steal your soul. Bare your soul at the next alumni
picnic by wearing your class picture on your chest.

Instructions

Convert a black-and-white portrait
into a rubber stamp by taking it to a
company that makes rubber stamps.
A photostamp is great for many
stamping crafts on fabric,
paper…whatever!

1 Practice using your stamp on
   paper before using it on fabric.
If you have a large rubber stamp
made, it might take a few tries to
determine the ink coverage and
pressure needed to stamp your
image. Place the scrap piece of
cardboard inside the T-shirt where
you want the image to appear. This
will keep ink and paint from soak-
ing through the material and stain-
ing the back of the T-shirt.

2 Stamp your image as many
   times as you wish on the front.
Allow it to dry.

3 Pour about a teaspoon of paint
   into a jar lid. Use the larger of
the two corks to stamp a "frame"
around the image. Allow the paint
to dry.

4 Pour about a teaspoon of your
   second color into a jar lid. Use
the smaller of the two corks to
stamp a second color on top of the
circles in the frame you made in
step 3. Allow the paint to dry.

5 Use an iron to heat-set the
   stamped image and frame.

Too Cool for School Portrait Card

DESIGNER: **TERRY TAYLOR**

Show how hip you've become by sending out personal notecards with a photostamp of you looking the way you did way back when. With the photostamp as your starting point, you can create many unique and unusual craft projects.

Materials

Rubber stamp made from a black-and-white photograph

Stamp pad

Blank greeting card and matching envelope

Gold paper doily

Glue stick

Tools

Scissors

Home computer with graphics software (optional)

Scanner (optional)

Instructions

1 Test the stamp on plain paper before using it on the card itself. If you had a large rubber stamp made, it may take you a few tries to determine the ink coverage and pressure needed to stamp your image. Ink the stamp completely, then stamp it onto the card.

2 Stamp your image as many times as you wish on the front. Allow it to dry.

3 Using scissors, cut out an opening in the center of the doily that is slightly larger than the stamped image.

4 Using a glue stick, adhere the doily to the front of the card, centering the opening over the stamped image.

Foxes & Hounds Box

DESIGNER: **DANA IRWIN**

Don't let your imagination stop at transferring photographic images
to paper and fabric alone. Snapshots taken at an equestrian event
were magically transferred to an ordinary wooden cigar box…
a great place to hold fireplace matches or blue ribbons.

Materials

Wooden box

Photographs

Transfer paper

Glue

Spray acrylic varnish

Matchsticks

Tools

Scissors

Iron

Instructions

The better the quality of the image
in the original photograph, the better the transfer will be. Avoid large
areas of dark shadows. Contrast
(bright highlights and definitive
shadow areas) and in-focus detail
are important.

1 If there are any areas in the
photographs that you really
don't want to use, trim these off.

2 Arrange and tape, or glue, as
many photos as you can fit onto
an 8½ x 11-inch (21.5 x 28 cm)
sheet of paper to use the transfer
paper material in the most efficient
way possible.

3 At a copy shop, have the color
copy duplicated onto the transfer paper.

4 First test the process using a
scrap piece of wood that is similar
to the box. The amount of time and
degree of pressure needed vary
according to the type of surface
you're transferring to. Iron the transfer, image side down, onto the wood,
holding the iron in contact with the
paper for 30 seconds. Move the iron
periodically, but do not slide the iron,
or the image will be blurry.

5 Wait 5 to 7 seconds after lifting
the iron to pull the paper off the
wood. If the paper doesn't come off
easily, repeat the process.

6 Glue the matchsticks onto the
edges of the box in a border design.

7 Spray with a clear or tinted
acrylic varnish.

POLYMER CLAY TRANSFERS

Try this unusual but easy transfer method using light-colored polymer clay and sharp, simple images.

Polymer clay is a wonderfully versatile material to use in decorative crafts, and it is quite simple to use. It's nontoxic when handled and baked correctly, and cleanup is easy, too.

Many artists work on a large sheet of glass, marble, clear plastic sheeting, or even a piece of waxed paper taped (with masking tape) to a table. Be sure to use only tools and equipment that you plan to dedicate to craft use. Many common kitchen items are wonderful for use with polymer clays, but don't ever use them for food again! A pasta machine is considered extremely useful in both proper conditioning of the clay and for rolling out thin, even sheets. If you don't want to make the investment in a pasta machine, a piece of PVC pipe, or acrylic roller or brayer, can be used instead.

It's important to use only properly conditioned clay for your projects, so be sure to follow the package instructions. Use a photocopied image with strong darks and lights, and use a light-colored—or even translucent—clay for the best contrast.

Photocopy your photograph, enlarging or reducing it to the size you wish the finished image to be. Using scissors, trim away excess paper from the image, cutting a small fold-up pull tab on one side.

Place the trimmed photocopy face down on the clay surface, centering it carefully and burnishing the image well. Make sure that the paper is making contact with the clay at all points, with no air bubbles underneath the sheet of paper, but don't press so hard that you disturb the smooth clay surface.

Place the clay and paper on a waxed-paper–covered baking sheet, and put it underneath a warm lamp for approximately 15 to 20 minutes to develop the transfer. When the transfer has developed, you will see a difference on the paper. It will have an oily look from the polymer clay leaching into the paper, and you will be able to see a faint outline of the image. Finally, bake it for approximately 20 minutes at the temperature indicated on the package of polymer clay. Allow the oven to cool down with the project inside. You may need to lay a weight (such as a small book) on the project during the cool-down phase to keep it from curling up at the edges. If you do so, place another sheet of wax paper between the project and the weight on top. Use this cool-down method in each of the projects that follow, always baking at the temperature recommended by the manufacturer.

With the simple process of transferring photos to polymer clay in these projects, you can either display a special shot, or use photographic images as decorative design elements in surprising ways. Polymer clay is so versatile, you'll find plenty of your own uses for this inventive technique.

Two Sisters Pin/Pendant

DESIGNER: **MICHELLE KIERNAN**

A favorite photo accented by gorgeous painted and embellished details becomes an elegant fashion statement with these photo-transferred polymer pins and pendants. They're sure to rival the vintage creations so popular in today's upscale boutiques.

Materials

Small black-and-white photograph

2 ounces (56 g) light-colored, conditioned polymer clay

2 ounces (56 g) black, conditioned polymer clay

Spool of 20-gauge craft wire (sterling silver, copper, brass, or anodized aluminum wire)

Tubing to fit your chain or cord (sterling silver, copper, aluminum, or clear plastic)

Chain or cord to hang pendant from

Acrylic iridescent paints in several colors (we used green, orange, violet, and blue)

Pin back or pin back/pendant bail

Tools

Scissors

Pasta machine, acrylic roller, or brayer

Waxed paper

Baking sheet

Craft knife

Rubber stamps or other texturing tools

Craft lamp or light

Toaster oven or kitchen oven

Small vise

Bent nail

Hand drill or power drill

Tube cutter or jewelry saw

400-grit and 600-grit sandpaper

Gel cyanoacrylate glue

White craft glue

Small paintbrush with stiff bristles

Paper towels

Instructions

Be sure to read the guidelines on handling, baking, and transferring images to the clay in Polymer Clay Transfers on page 110.

1 Using a pasta machine, acrylic roller, or brayer, roll out a small quantity of the light-colored polymer clay to create a thin, even sheet of clay. Place the sheet on a piece of wax paper. Then, place this on the baking pan.

2 Prepare a photocopied image and transfer it to the clay sheet. Remove the paper carefully, so as not to disturb the image on the surface of the clay.

3 Using a craft knife, trim the clay to the size you wish the finished image to be. Place the baking pan in the oven and bake it according to the temperature indicated on the package of polymer clay. Bake the piece for approximately 15 minutes; allow it to cool down.

4 Using a pasta machine, acrylic roller, or brayer, roll out a thin sheet of conditioned black polymer clay. Place it on a sheet of wax paper. Create a textured surface on the black clay by using one or more rubber stamps pressed into the surface. This sheet will be used to make the frame for your baked image.

5 Place the baked image face up on the textured sheet. Using a craft knife, trace around the baked image. Remove the baked image and, using the craft knife, lift up the middle, cut-out section of the textured background, leaving a hole where the baked image fits. Place the baked image into the hole. Use the craft knife to trim the background sheet to make your final pendant shape.

NOTE: If you are making a pin, bake the frame with the prebaked image for approximately 15 minutes. Then, proceed to step 10. If, however, you are making a twisted wire bail for a pendant, continue with step 6.

MAKING A WIRE BAIL

6 Take a 4-foot (1.22 m) piece of wire, and fold it in half. Put the two free ends of the folded wire into the jaws of a small vise, and tighten the vise to hold the wire. Attach the folded end of the doubled length of wire to a bent nail or cup hook placed in a hand drill. Hold the drill and pull the wire taut, but not too tightly, then wind the crank of the hand drill. The wire will twist. When the wire has been twisted, remove the wire from both the drill and the vise. You can also use a power drill with a bent nail or cup hook in its jaws to twist the wire; just be sure to operate it at a low speed!

7 Use pliers to make a right angled bend in the end of the wire. Use this angled bend as a tail and begin to wrap the wire securely around a length of tubing. When the coil is slightly shorter than the top of your pendant, stop wrapping the tubing, again leaving a short tail at the bottom. Your coil should sit on a flat surface with the two tails supporting it, as in figure 1.

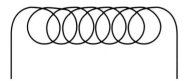

Figure 1

8 Cut the tubing to the desired length, using the tube cutter or jewelry saw. Using the 400-grit sandpaper, lightly sand the cut edge(s) of the tubing. Next, using the 600-grit sandpaper, lightly sand smooth the edge of the tubing.

9 Place the twisted-wire bail you have just created under the top of your unbaked pendant frame, where it will ultimately lie. Bake as indicated in step 3 above, again noting that it may be necessary to weight the piece during cool-down in the oven.

10 Roll out more well-conditioned black clay, this time into a thicker sheet. Remove the twisted-wire bail from underneath the baked piece if you are making a pendant. Place the baked piece face up on top of the sheet of raw black clay, cutting around the entire pendant with your blade or knife. Make two of these unbaked pendant-shaped black pieces.

11 Turn the baked piece onto its back, coat the back with white glue, and allow it to dry. With the baked piece still on its back, replace the twisted wire bail at the top of the back and place a dot of gel cyanoacrylate glue onto each of the "legs" of the bail, where they project down onto the back of the pendant. If you are

making a pin, coat the back of your baked piece with white glue and allow it to dry.

12 Place one pendant-size piece of raw black clay onto the glue-covered back of the baked piece, smoothing it gently into place. Use your fingers to gently smooth all seams, and make sure that there is no air trapped between the layers of raw and baked clay. Then, add the second pendant-size piece of raw black clay to the back of the pendant and smooth it into place.

13 Carefully place your pendant/pin on the baking sheet lined with a piece of waxed paper, and bake again at approximately 265°F (130°C) for 30 to 40 minutes, on the baking sheet. Allow the piece to cool down in the oven.

14 After the piece is removed from the oven, paint the frame to highlight the surface texture. Use the dark paint first, making sure to push the paint in the deep crevices of the texture pattern. Then take a lightly moistened piece of paper towel and go over the piece, removing most of the paint, but leaving it in the crevices of the texture. Next, paint small highlight areas of the frame with the lighter paint, using the lightly-moistened paper towel to remove most of it.

Decorative Light Switch Plate

DESIGNER: **MICHELLE KIERNAN**

Simple switch plates usually go unnoticed, so why not transform them into attractive decorative accents, and show off some favorite photos, too? With easy-to-find materials and a few easy-to-follow steps, you'll soon be adding your own special touches to switch plates, outlet covers, and more!

Instructions

Be sure to read the guidelines on handling, baking, and transferring images to the clay in Polymer Clay Transfers on page 84.

1 Select a switch plate to fit your wall fixture. Coat the top surface of the switch plate with a thick application of craft glue, then allow it to dry.

2 Use a pasta machine, roller, or brayer to make a thin even sheet.

3 Place the sheet on top of the switch plate, rubbing from the center outward with your thumbs to adhere it to the plate. If you find trapped air bubbles, piece them with the craft knife; press the bubble flat, then smooth the clay surface to remove the blade marks.

4 Using the craft knife, trim around the edge of the switch plate to remove the excess clay. Then, working from the back of the switch plate, cut out the opening for the switch.

5 Turn the piece over and neaten up the cuts around the opening, removing the clay from these sections. A small tool with square sides, such as a chopstick, is perfect for squaring up the sides of the opening.

6 Working from the front of the switch plate, use the end of a small paintbrush to push through the holes where the screws will attach the plate to the wall.

7 Transfer the photocopied image to the clay. Keep in mind that a switch plate generally has a flat center and sloping or angled sides. The photocopy should be sized to fit within the flat area only.

8 After the plate has been removed from the oven and is still slightly warm, remove the paper from the surface of the clay. Carefully pry up an edge with a knife, then slowly peel back the paper.

9 To highlight the textured areas of the plate, paint over the entire clay surface. Using a small, stiff paintbrush, push the paint down into the deep crevices of the texture pattern. Then, with a lightly moistened piece of paper towel, go over the part you just painted, removing most of the paint, but leaving it down in the crevices of the texture.

10 Attach the switch plate to the wall. Because of the thicker polymer clay surface, it may be necessary to use longer screws than your switch plate originally required.

Materials

Light switch plate in metal, wood, nylon, or plastic

White craft glue

Paper towels

4 ounces (112 g) light-colored, conditioned polymer clay

Photocopies of small, good-quality, black-and-white images or contact sheets

Piece of blank paper

Acrylic paint (any color that coordinates with your project; burnt umber was used here)

Tools

Pasta machine, acrylic roller, or brayer

Craft knife

Chopstick or small tool with square sides

Small paintbrush with stiff bristles

Scissors

Dull kitchen knife

Wax paper

Baking sheet

Craft lamp or light

Toaster oven or kitchen oven

Screwdriver

Materials

Powdered fabric dye
(several colors)

Unfinished wood box or vessel
in a medium or large size

Small black-and-white photo-
graphs(s)

2 ounces (56 g) light-colored,
conditioned polymer clay

2 ounces (56 g) dark-colored,
conditioned polymer clay

Decorative or handmade papers

Acrylic paint

Optional: wire mesh, beads, jewelry
bits and parts, buttons, three-
dimensional or fabric paint

Tools

Sponge

Scissors

Pasta machine, acrylic roller,
or brayer

Craft knife

Wax paper

Baking sheet

Craft lamp or light

Toaster oven or kitchen oven

Rubber stamps or other
texturing tools

White craft glue

Small paintbrush with stiff bristles

Large foam brush

Paper towels

Gel cyanoacrylate glue

Collaged
Desk Caddies

DESIGNER: **MICHELLE KIERNAN**

Decorated with bright paint and whimsical adornments, these small boxes brighten any desk or countertop. At work or in the home office, they hold everything from pens and pencils to mail and scrap paper.

Instructions

Be sure to read the guidelines on handling, baking, and transferring images to the clay in Polymer Clay Transfers on page 84.

1 First, mix a solution using the powdered dye and water, about 2 tablespoons of dye to $\frac{1}{4}$ cup (59 mL) of water. You can experiment to get a consistency you like, testing the dye solution on extra small wooden cubes or beads. Mix your own colors, or use the dye right out of the package. Using a sponge or large foam brush, apply a small quantity of the dye solution to the wooden pieces, using a wiping motion. A small amount provides good coverage. As an alternative method of application, submerge the wooden pieces in the dye solution. Dry them on a paper towel. Repeat the application as often as necessary to achieve the desired color. Any unused dye solution can be stored in a tightly capped plastic container.

2 Roll out a small quantity of the light-colored polymer clay to make a thin, even sheet of clay. Place the sheet of clay on a baking pan covered with wax paper.

3 Transfer the photocopied image to the clay sheet. Remove the paper carefully so as not to disturb the image on the surface of the clay.

4 Using a craft knife, trim the clay to the size that you wish the finished image to be. You can also use a cookie cutter to trim the shape. Bake the piece for approximately 10 minutes at the temperature indicated on the package of polymer clay; let it cool in the oven.

5 Roll out a similar thickness of dark polymer clay with the pasta machine or roller. Place it on a sheet of wax paper. Create a textured surface on the clay by pressing one or more rubber stamps (or other texturing tools) into the surface. This sheet of clay will be used to make the frame for your baked image.

6 Place the image you already baked face up on the textured sheet of raw clay. Using a craft knife, trace around the baked image. Remove the baked image and, using a small sharp tool, lift up the middle, cut-out section of the textured background, leaving a hole where the baked image fits. Place the baked image into the cutout.

7 Using the knife, trim the background sheet to make the final frame shape. Then bake again at the temperature indicated on the clay package, this time increasing the baking time to 20 to 30 minutes. Allow the oven to cool down with the project inside.

8 Tear or cut several small pieces of decorative paper or wire mesh into progressively smaller pieces; these will be background pieces for your baked image. To see how your collage looks, first lay the layers down on your workspace without glue. Put the largest one down first, then the next largest on top of it. Continue until you are satisfied with the design.

9 Once you have your collage laid out, begin with the bottom (largest) piece. Turn it front side down and apply a thin, even coat of craft glue to the back with a large foam brush. Put the bottom layer on the front of your box, smoothing it down from the center out to eliminate any air bubbles.

Nostalgic Treasure Box

DESIGNER:
MICHELLE KIERNAN

With a few easy decorative techniques, this simple wooden box becomes a lovely place to store your old keepsakes, jewelry, even cherished love letters. Whatever decoration you wish to add—from saved paper scraps to simple found objects—they'll all help this become a personal item cherished for years to come.

Materials

Powdered fabric dye
  (several colors)

Unfinished wood box or vessel
  in a medium or large size

Unfinished wood cubes or
  square/round unfinished
  wooden beads

Small black-and-white photo-
  graph(s)

2 ounces (56 g) light-colored,
  conditioned polymer clay

2 ounces (56 g) dark-colored,
  conditioned polymer clay

Decorative or handmade papers

Acrylic paint

Optional: wire mesh, beads,
  jewelry bits and parts,
  buttons, three-dimensional
  or fabric paint

Tools

Sponge

Scissors

Pasta machine, acrylic roller,
  or brayer

Craft knife

Wax paper

Baking sheet

Craft lamp or light

Toaster oven or kitchen oven

Rubber stamps or other
  texturing tools

White craft glue

Small paintbrush with stiff bristles

Large foam brush

Paper towels

Gel cyanoacrylate glue

Instructions

Be sure to read the guidelines on handling, baking, and transferring images to the clay in Polymer Clay Transfers on page 84.

1 Mix the solution as described in step 1 on page 116.

2 Roll out a small quantity of the light-colored polymer clay to make a thin, even sheet. Place the sheet of clay on a baking pan lined with wax paper.

3 Transfer the photocopied image to the sheet of clay. Take care not to disturb the image on the surface of the clay when removing the photocopy.

4 Using a craft knife or even a cookie cutter, trim the clay to the size that you wish the finished image to be. Bake the piece for approximately 10 minutes at the temperature indicated on the package of polymer clay, then allow it to cool down inside the oven.

5 Roll out a similar thickness of dark polymer clay with the pasta machine or roller. Place it on a sheet of wax paper. Create a textured surface on the clay by pressing one or more rubber stamps (or other texturing tools) into the surface. This sheet of clay will be used to make the frame for your baked image.

6 Place the image you already baked face up on the textured sheet of raw clay. Using a craft knife, trace around the baked image. Remove the baked image and, using a small sharp tool, lift up the middle, cutout section of the textured background, leaving a hole where the baked image fits. Place the baked image into the cutout.

7 Using the knife, trim the background sheet to make the final frame shape. Then, bake again at the temperature indicated on the clay package, this time increasing the baking time to approximately 20 to 30 minutes. Allow the oven to cool down with the project inside.

8 Tear or cut several small pieces of decorative paper or wire mesh into progressively smaller pieces; these will be background pieces for your baked image. To see how your collage looks, lay the layers down on your workspace without glue. Put the largest one down first, then the next largest on top of it. Continue until you are satisfied with the design.

9 Once you have your collage laid out, begin with the bottom (largest) piece. Turn it front side down and apply a thin even coat of craft glue to the back with a large foam brush. Place this piece on the front of the box, smoothing it down from the center out to eliminate any air bubbles.

10 Continue applying glue to the back side of each of your collage elements and pressing the items onto the front of the box, ending with the baked polymer piece and the frame. Allow the glue to dry.

11 To make "feet" for the box, take the wooden cubes or beads that were dyed earlier, and place a small dot of the gel cyanoacrylate glue on one of the surfaces of each cube. Place the box upside down, bottom up. Position each of the feet on the bottom of the box. Allow the glue to dry before proceeding to the next step.

12 While the glue is drying, coat one of the unfinished wooden cubes or beads with craft glue. Allow it to dry.

13 While the glue is drying on the wooden cube or bead, construct a base for the lid's handle. Form a thin patty of conditioned black clay, and flatten it into a circular shape. Then, use a rubber stamp or texturing tool to create a textured pattern. Set this aside for the moment.

14 Cut four small square-shaped pieces of the same light-colored clay you used to make your photo transfer. The squares should fit onto the sides and top of the square cube you coated with glue in step 12. Press them onto the square, using gentle pressure to

adhere them. Using rubber stamps or other texturing tools, stamp designs onto the sides and/or top of the clay-covered cube.

15 Roll a tiny bead of the conditioned black clay between your palms. Carefully press it onto the top of the clay-covered cube. Place the cube onto the round base you made in step 13, and bake the whole handle for approximately 20 to 30 minutes at the temperature indicated on the clay package. Let it stay in the oven until the oven has cooled.

16 Using a stiff brush, apply acrylic paint to the handle, making sure the paint gets down into the crevices of the texture. Then, use a lightly moistened paper towel to remove most of the paint. Finally, coat the bottom with a generous coat of craft glue. Let it dry to a tacky stage.

17 Meanwhile, tear or cut some coordinating pieces of decorative or handmade paper into small pieces to place underneath the handle on top of the box. Glue each piece into position on the top of the box, then glue the handle into position.

18 As a final decorative step, you may wish to embellish the box in other ways. Glue on small items such as beads, bits of old jewelry, or other found items, or stamp decorative borders onto the edges of the box.

CRAFTING WITH DIGITAL PHOTOGRAPHS

Computers and digital cameras offer wonderful new possibilities for making photographs and creating craft projects from them. You can now send your film to a processor, receive an e-mail link to your picture files, then send them to family and friends in an e-mail or on a Web page—all before you get the film and prints back in the mail. More and more, digital options are being offered in all the familiar places where you've always had your film developed, whether at a photo processor, a drugstore, or a discount mart. Don't forget: when it comes to digital crafting, you have plenty of choices.

HOW TO MAKE A DIGITAL PHOTOGRAPH

There are basically two ways to get a picture into the computer: take a photograph with a digital camera (perhaps we'll coin it "digitography"), or convert a traditional photographic print into an electronic data file with a scanner. With either method, you'll want to know how to get high resolution for the sharpest possible pictures.

Resolution, Resolution, Resolution

If there's one important technical fact to keep in mind, it's the degree of sharpness, or resolution, your digital devices can produce. Digital images are made up of many tiny squares, called pixels. The greater the resolution, the smaller the squares and the more information can be packed into the picture: more detail, more subtle color and tonal variations, sharper pictures. The computer screen, the digital camera, the scanner, and the printer—each one's resolution is expressed in either pixels-per-inch (ppi) or dots-per-inch (dpi).

In order to create sharp printouts with plenty of detail, you'll need plenty of resolution, and in order for the computer to handle all that information, you'll need plenty of memory, speed, and storage space. Of course, the more your computer or camera can do, the higher the purchase price.

Digital Photographs from Prints

You can take pictures on regular film with any 35 millimeter camera, have a photo processor develop the film, make the prints, and then scan, or digitize, your pictures, too. The photo processor then puts them onto a CD for you to use in your computer, and sometimes, as a free service, stores them on their Web

Computer, flatbed scanner, and a digital camera convert photographic images into pixels.

Images of Blackberry Farm, in North Carolina, were taken with a digital camera and inkjet-printed on plain, 20-lb. paper. *Photos by George W. Beeler, Jr.*

site, too. From there, you can download them to your home computer.

To use images from existing prints, first get them digitized. Either have a full-service photocopy shop, camera store, or photographic services shop do the job for you, or you can scan them yourself (see Types of Scanners). When you have someone else scan your pictures, they'll put the files onto an electronic storage medium, such as a ZIP disk, so you can view and print them at home or at a shop (for more information on digital file storage, see The Traveling Picture File on page 98).

There's no need to rush right out and buy a lot of new equipment to be able to use photographs on the computer, as long as the equipment and software you do have is reasonably up to date.

Digital Photographs from a Digital Camera

If you'd like to bypass film processing and having prints digitized, think about using a fun new digital camera instead. Digital cameras look a lot like point-and-shoot cameras, but the picture is stored on a floppy disk or memory card of some sort instead of film. Buying extra cards—just like buying extra film—means you're less likely to run out of space on the camera for your pictures.

When it comes to crafting, if you're aiming for a really nice, sharp, photographic quality image, just go ahead and invest in the highest-resolution camera you can afford. When shopping for a filmless camera, look for the word "megapixel;" this describes the camera's ability to record as much detail as possible.

The price for cameras with a low image resolution of, say, 640 x 480 pixels, has dropped dramatically, but those pictures are meant to be used in e-mails and on web sites, and not printed out. Shop instead for mega-resolution, which gives you great printouts, even though they're not yet as clear, rich, and sharp as film-based images. The rock-bottom–priced "web only" cameras also have very few special features, which means you don't have as much control over what the camera does.

The LCD display available on the mid-priced cameras is a great feature. This lets you preview your shot on a tiny viewer. If you don't like the digital picture you just took, just delete it and try again. No more wasted film, no more disappointments when the prints come

back. When you have the pictures you want, download them from the camera to the computer (you can only store a few high-resolution pictures on a single memory card). Avoid a digital camera with a serial port computer connector cord for the download connection to your computer. Instead, go for the latest Universal Serial Bus (USB) port— it's faster and will probably replace cord-type connectors altogether, in the near future.

Types of Scanners

The flatbed scanner, though not essential, is a versatile tool for digitizing photos as well as all sorts of other flat things. A scanner capable of rendering at least 2,400 dpi in 30-bit color can capture all the subtle gradations of tone and fine detail of a good photographic print. Although sheet scanners have limited capabilities in size and resolving power, their lower price makes them a good bet for the beginner computer crafter. With your own scanner, you can digitize all your old photographic prints—but scanning negatives and slides requires a special kind of film scanner or adapter.

Remember that a full-service copy or photographic services shop can do your print, negative, and slide scanning for you. The advantage of using a shop, instead of investing in your own scanner, is that their equipment is usually the very latest that's available.

Software Solutions

Compared to the other parts of the digital trail, software can be relatively cheap—even free, when you buy a computer, camera, or scanner. There's also some great freeware available online—just be sure to scan it for viruses before downloading and installing it! All these programs have basic features once found only in a real darkroom, such as cropping, resizing, and rotating; correction features for color balance and red-eye; plus all kinds of special effects such as stretching and cutouts. Floral Glass Coasters (page 111) uses a soft-edged vignette that is commonly available in picture software programs. Some programs will even let you instantly change a color photo into a romantic, vintage-like black-and-white picture.

The Traveling Picture File

If you want to carry your digital file to a copy shop for a color laser print, you'll need a type of storage medium big enough to hold it. If there is a drawback to all this business about resolution, it's the issue of file size. The higher the resolution, the better your output qual-

ity, but then the larger the file will be. The bigger the file, the more powerful the computer itself must be to run the picture software. Keep in mind that portable, high-resolution files take up a lot of memory. You'll soon need a ZIP disk or a read/write CD to keep plenty of space open on the hard drive for running the software. Floppy disks are quickly phasing out—a good indicator that their storage capacity isn't practical for today's computing needs.

Format It

Remember VHS and Beta video-tape formats? You had to commit to one or the other, because a Beta tape just wouldn't play on a VHS machine, and vice versa. File format decisions are similar to that dilemma. If you save your files in a format that is compatible with most software and hardware, and one that delivers high-quality prints, your print jobs will be just as simple to do on a retail-business color laser printer as they are at home on your inkjet printer.

Not all file formats deliver the same print quality—in fact, some (such as JPEG) are not meant to be printed at all. Take into account what software and which printer or printers you'll be using when making these decisions. Read your software and printer documentation to find out what your options are. At present, the TIFF file format is recognized by all major software programs, whether on a Windows or Macintosh operating system.

Run a simple test to find out which file format gives you the results you want for your output source (inkjet printer or laser printer). Do this by importing a high-resolution image into the picture software, then saving it at a resolution appropriate to that printer. You might try this with each of the file format options your software offers, always beginning with the hi res image file, and keeping a record of the settings you used.

Some programs, as well as the pictures that come from the photo processor on a CD, have a proprietary file format option. Beware; this is probably not a universally recognized format. You may be saving your picture in a special computer language that only that particular software can read. Use this file format only if you plan to print exclusively at home. If you took a file of this type to a copy shop for a laser print, it would be like to taking your Beta-format video cassette over to your friend's VHS-type videotape player. To be safe, save images in the TIFF file format.

Once an image is digitized, there's really no limit to where you can go with it. AnnaCat Digital Greeting Card (page 101) was created from a hybrid of digital-camera and traditional photographic prints, collaged together in a computer "darkroom" program. With an understanding of the basics of digital image making, it's time to look at basic and creative options for printing. The next section covers how to get the best, technically and imaginatively, from your digital files.

PRINTING A DIGITAL FILE

Whether you're at home, working with a technician, or renting time at a self-serve computer, there probably will be some trial and error in printing digital files. Go ahead and experiment a little. If you get something you really do or don't like, write down the settings you used, so that you can repeat it—or avoid it—later on.

Check your inkjet printer's manual, or call the copy shop where you'll be printing out your pictures and ask them for the resolution of both their color and black-and-white laser printers. In general, scan and/or create digital photos at a resolution setting one-half that of your intended output device. For example, when you know you'll be using a printer with a resolution of 720 dpi, create and/or save the image files at 360.

Corrina and Deborah were snapped with a megapixel digital camera and printed on photo-quality inkjet paper. Megapixel quality is beginning to approach that of traditional prints. *Photo by Esther Holsen*

Inkjet Printing

Specialty papers, such as colored stock, pattern-printed, and "photographic" papers, are all readily available; these are fairly lightweight, but the inks themselves are not waterproof or lightfast. Various formats of card stock and pre-scored greeting cards and envelopes are also available. You can even print your own fabric transfers on an inkjet printer if you like (for more information, turn to the section From Image to Fabric and More, page 62). Keep in mind that colored paper will alter the color of color images and change your design. The ink is

transparent and blends with the paper color, rather than covering it.

Try exotic papers from an art supply store when you're ready to experiment a little. Keep in mind that hard-surfaced papers will hold the ink better, and check with the printer manual in case thicker papers require an adjustment of the inkjet printer head. The Wilderness Hike Digital Photo Journal (page 116) was printed on an inkjet printer using medium-weight watercolor paper, and bound into a beautiful book.

The printer software allows you to adjust the size of the paper, and

the picture software lets you control the size and placement of the image within that paper size; this area is sometimes called the *canvas*. For the inkjet printer, you may want to use a "draft" or "quick" mode the first time around. Printing to a paper size larger than the final product allows you to put a pencil mark at the top of the paper, for duplex (double-sided) printing, or when printing on a deckle edge paper. The excess paper can be trimmed off later. The printers' software may include templates for different envelope sizes, too.

STANDARD PAPER SIZES

FOR PHOTOCOPIERS, INKJET, AND LASER PRINTERS:

LETTER
8½ x 11 inches (A4 or 27.9 x 21 cm)

LEGAL
8½ x 14 inches (21 x 35.5 cm)

LEDGER
11 x 17 inches (A3 or 42 x 27.9 cm)

When printing both the front and back of a piece of paper with an inkjet printer, it may not track precisely the same each time through the printer. Leaving large margins to allow for error will help. Or you can print your files on separate sheets and glue them together, back to back. If you use a coated "photo quality" inkjet paper, you may want to do this anyway, so you'll have a finished look on both sides. Because of the special nature of the process, printing on both sides of a single sheet of paper is not recommended for laser printers.

Laser Printing at the Copy Shop

A full-service copy shop offers a wealth of possibilities to the general crafter. In addition to color and black-and-white photocopiers, they offer access to design stations that include top-notch computers, scanners, and both color and black-and-white printers. There is no end to what a full-service store can do.

Black-and-white laser printers use dry toner similar to that used in a photocopy machine. Toner is transferred to the paper using heat and pressure. Laser prints look great and are relatively inexpensive, but it will probably be the copy shop, not you, who chooses the paper, because these printers are finicky, taking only 20- to 80-lb. (9 to 36 kg) papers. The Celebrity Look Gift Box and Bag on page 48 shows a great way to use colored paper to punch up a black-and-white laser-printed design. Color laser prints are more expensive than black-and-white ones.

The technicians at these shops have more time for questions and unusual requests during off-peak hours, but most of these businesses are understandably reluctant to send handmade papers through their machines—loose fibers can cause jams and even fires in the high-temperature environment of a laser copier. If you do want to print on them, the papers are usually sold in big sheets, 20 x 30 inches (50.75 x 76.25 cm) or larger; cut them down to standard sizes.

Now you have all the information you need to begin making impressive papercrafts that delight the eye. Everyone will be asking how you became a computer whiz when they see the creativity that's possible with pixels and printouts.

AnnaCat
Digital Greeting Card   DESIGNER: **ESTHER HOLSEN**

This playful collage uses digital-camera images of a little girl named Anna and a whimsical wooden cat, plus 35 millimeter snapshots of backyard coneflowers. The secret to collecting material for collage is to look for color, texture, size, and subject matter that both complement and contrast each other. Collage is a method that often surprises the viewer with its unusual juxtapositions.

Materials

Digital photographic images*

10 x 7-inch (25.5 x 17.75 cm) card stock, or standard letter-size paper

Envelope to hold 5 x 7-inch (12.75 x 17.75 cm) folded card

Tools

Computer with plenty of available memory (follow software manufacturer's recommendations)

Photo-editing computer software

Inkjet color printer

Digital camera and/or scanner (or access to a scanner)

* The designer used a combination of images from a digital camera and scanned photographic prints. Use digitized images from any source available to you: digital camera, film processing service, or scanner. See Crafting with Digital Photographs on page 96, for more information.

Instructions

To create a collage, the software should have selection tools and a layer, or stacking, function; check your manual or help file. This project demands a lot from your computer's memory. As much speed and space on your computer as you can muster will make it more fun.

1 Name a new folder on your hard drive for the project (the designer called hers "AnnaCat").

2 Gather together the images you wish to use, in digital form. They can be made directly from a digital camera or from scanned photographic prints. If they come from a digital camera, they will already be in JPEG file format. Save scanned images in the TIFF format. Put them all in the folder. If you like, print out the digital images and photocopy the prints, so you can try out different compositions.

3 To make the outside of the card, open a new file in the software and give it the correct dimensions (sometimes called the *canvas* size): 10 x 7 inches (25.5 x 17.75 cm). Name the file "Outside" or another name that identifies it; this is where most of your work will go. The right-hand half of the canvas area will be the display part of the card, and the left-hand side will be the outside back (where a logo might go). You'll make another file for the inside of the card.

4 Retrieve the background image from the AnnaCat folder, and place it on the right half of the card. Resize it, using the cropping, trimming, or image-resize tools. Reposition the image until it sits in the center of the right half, with a generous and even border all around. This can all be adjusted and fine-tuned later. Save your work.

5 Photograph a small object with a digital camera (here the designer used a carved wood cat figure) on a plain paper background called *seamless* (see How to Make a Seamless Background). Use a color wand tool or an automatic-selection tool to select the entire one-color background all at once. Then either delete the selected background, or invert the selection, so the cat is selected, and cut-and-paste it into the Outside file. This is a lot easier than using a tracing tool, but the tracing tool is another option. Use color adjusting options as desired; the designer made the cat a brighter yellow, to better complement the background colors. Save your work.

6 If your image has a busy, complicated background, use a trace tool to separate the subject from the unwanted elements. Tracing is more time-consuming, but it provides very precise results. Zoom in on the area you're working on, if that is an option, for greater precision.

7 When you have the all the picture elements you want, place them on the background. In order to establish the best composition, move them around on the screen, or use printed-out pictures to plan the design in advance. On the screen, you will be able to resize, flip, multiply, distort, and otherwise enhance them. Stacking and overlapping images gives greater depth to the image. If you have a layers or stacking option, merge all the picture elements after you have the final composition. This dramatically reduces the size of the file.

8 To make the frame, select a flower and duplicate it, along with several oval and rectangular bits of the collaged central image, then arrange them into a border motif. Trace a small detail from one of the digital images to use as a design motif in each of the corners.

9 If you wish, place a logo or scanned signature in the left half of the canvas area, which is the back of the card. Use the software's text capacity to include a name, date, place, or other personal information. Doing so creates a nice surprise element in the overall design of the card and gives it a very finished look.

10 For the inside of the card, make another new file with the same dimensions as the outside. Traditionally, the left-hand half of the inside of the card is blank, but the right-hand side can have some decoration while leaving room for a handwritten message. Here, the child, the cat, and cutout copies of the left-hand flower, duplicated three times, were used (see inset).

11 Printing is sure to involve some trial and error. It is probably best to use the draft mode the first time around. If the file was set up for a larger paper size, the 10 x 7-inch (25.5 x 17.75 cm) image area will be surrounded by extra paper that needs trimming all around. This extra area can be helpful when you need to print on both sides of a page. Mark an X at the top and right edges of the paper to determine how to put it back in the printer so the printing on the other side will be correctly oriented.

HOW TO MAKE A SEAMLESS BACKGROUND

If you've ever wanted to photograph a single object without getting a lot of confusing details in the picture, try this professional photographer's tip: use plain paper to make a background that the pros call *seamless*. Start with a large (at least 24-inch [61 cm]) piece of plain paper—any kind of paper that comes in a roll will do. Tape the paper at the edge, near the top of a medium-sized box, so that it curves down onto the tabletop, extending out at least 12 inches (30.5 cm).

Smiling Angels Pillow

DESIGNER: **ROBERTA BATES**

The Smiling Angels of Rheims beam down on all who visit that remarkable Gothic cathedral. The 35 millimeter snapshots taken on this memorable trip were immortalized in this wonderful, easy-to-sew pillow set. Transform your own memories of a special time into an elegant display.

Instructions

1 Scan (or have scanned) a glossy photographic print and use computer graphic software to give the image an artistic border. Following the manufacturer's instructions for the fabric transfer sheet brand that you use, print the image onto the sheet and then transfer it onto the 8 x 10 (20 x 25 cm) fabric. An alternative is to have a copy shop transfer the photographic image onto the cloth for you. Use the same cotton-blend broadcloth for the transfer as you use for the material for the pillow cover.

2 Determine how much extra fabric you want to extend around the fabric transfer, then add a $1/2$-inch (1.25 cm) seam allowance. Cut to the desired size. From the wrong side of the fabric, press under the seam allowance.

3 For the front of the pillow cover, measure, mark, and cut one square 19 x 19 inches (48.25 x 48.25 cm) on the straight grain of the $5/8$ (.55 m) yard of fabric. This includes a $1/2$-inch (1.25 cm) seam allowance.

4 For the back of the pillow cover, measure and cut one square 19 x 20 inches (48.25 x 50.75 cm) along the straight grain of the fabric. This includes a $1/2$-inch (1.25 cm) seam allowance, plus 1 inch (2.5 cm) for the zipper casing.

5 Center the photo transfer on the front of the 19 x 19-inch (48.25 cm) square, pinning it into place with straight pins. Topstitch this very closely to the transfer's folded edges.

6 Place the cording on the right side of the front pillow cover with the raw edges together. Using a zipper foot and a long machine stitch, baste the cording to the right side of the front pillow cover, curving the stitch at the corners, as shown in figure 1.

7 Cut the back piece of the pillow cover into two pieces for insertion of the zipper (see figure 2).

8 Turn in $1/2$ inch (1.25 cm) of the two pieces you just cut, and press. Put the zipper, with the zipper pull exposed, under the two folded and pressed edges of the back pieces. Using a zipper foot, topstitch the zipper into place, or follow the directions printed on the zipper package.

9 Pin the right side of the front pillow cover to the right side of the back pillow cover. Stitch all four sides, curving all the corners slightly as you did for the cording.

10 Turn the pillow cover right side out, and insert the pillow form into the finished pillow cover.

Materials

FOR ONE 18-INCH (45.75 CM) PILLOW

Photocopy of your photograph

Photo transfer sheet

Cotton-blend broadcloth, 8 x 10 inches (20 x 25 cm)

$5/8$ yard (.55 m) of 54-inch (137 cm) ecru-colored cotton/rayon blend broadcloth

1 zipper, 18 inches (45.75 cm) long

Spool of matching thread

1 foam pillow form, 18 inches square (45.75 cm)

2 yards (1.75 m) of fabric-covered cording

Tools

Computer

Graphics software

Scanner (or access to a scanner)

Printer

Sewing machine

Straightedge

Scissors

Iron

Fabric-marking tool

Straight pins

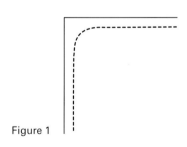

Figure 1

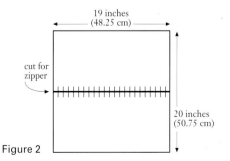

Figure 2

Celebrity Look
Gift Box and Bag

DESIGNER: **SUSAN KINNEY**

Your face may not be on the silver screen, but it gets movie-star treatment in this digital project. A color photograph was radically cropped, changed into a black-and-white image, then printed on colored card stock for a glamorous, posterized look. You can even make a tiny, folded gift tag with the leftover paper.

Materials

Black-and-white photograph, any size

White $8^{1}/_{2}$ x 11-inch (A4 or 27.9 x 21 cm) laser printer paper

Colored $8^{1}/_{2}$ x 11-inch (A4 or 27.9 x 21 cm) laser printer card stock, matte or glossy surface

Tools

Computer

Graphics software

Scanner (or access to a scanner)

Black-and-white laser printer

Scissors

Bone folder

Instructions

1 Pick an appropriate image for a gift box or bag. Start with a digital image, scan a favorite photographic print, or have a service scan it for you. If you intend to crop or significantly enlarge the image, be sure to scan it as a high resolution file.

2 If necessary, use photo imaging software to crop the print. Extreme cropping—using a small part of a larger image—simplifies any image, leaving just a few important details. Adjust the size, if necessary, to one that is proportionate to the size of the bag or box you're making.

3 You may leave the image as is, or, if the software has this option, change the print into a black-and-white or a sepia tone. Use a darker paper to print black-and-white images; they'll look better. When you're pleased with the color, select and copy the image. This keeps a duplicate of the image in an invisible holding area, or "clipboard," in the computer's memory.

4 Scan one of the templates from page 108 or 109. Name the scan "box template" or "bag template." Save the file.

5 Open a new image file. Access the scanned template. Scale the template to the desired size, then print the template onto plain white paper with the laser printer. For a larger bag or box, you can print it in one or more parts, then join them at the seams with a glue stick.

6 Paste the photo images into different areas, all over the canvas area. This area corresponds to the size of the paper you intend to print on. Use your own artistic judgment and creativity for placement. Try turning some of the copies sideways or upside down, or use reversed images if the software allows it.

7 Print on either matte-surface or shiny card stock.

8 Cut out the template with scissors. Fold the printed card stock, using the template as a guide. Glue the seams shut with a glue stick, using a bone folder to press and smooth them down.

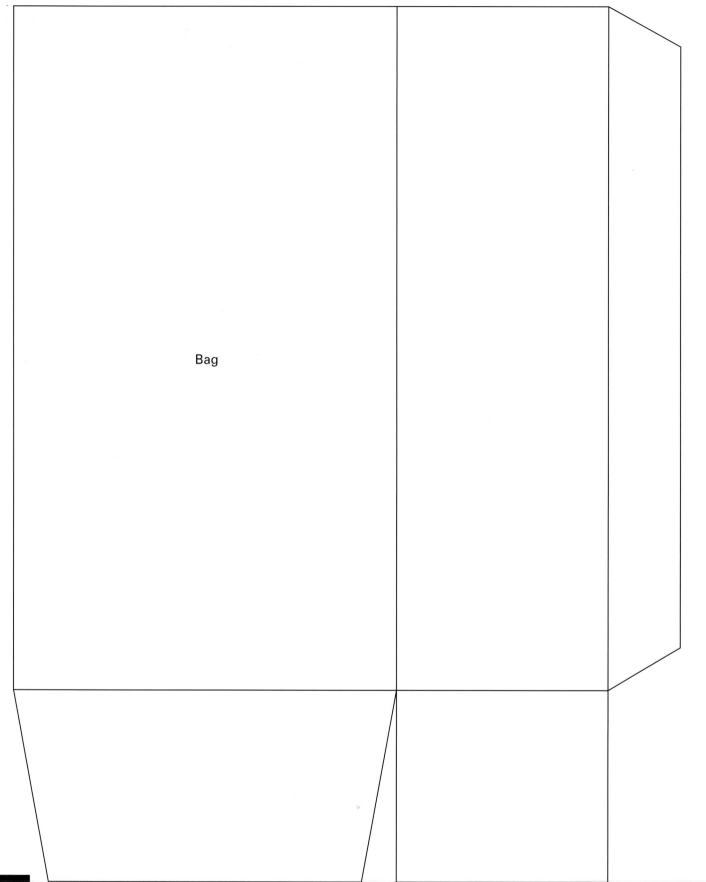

Bag

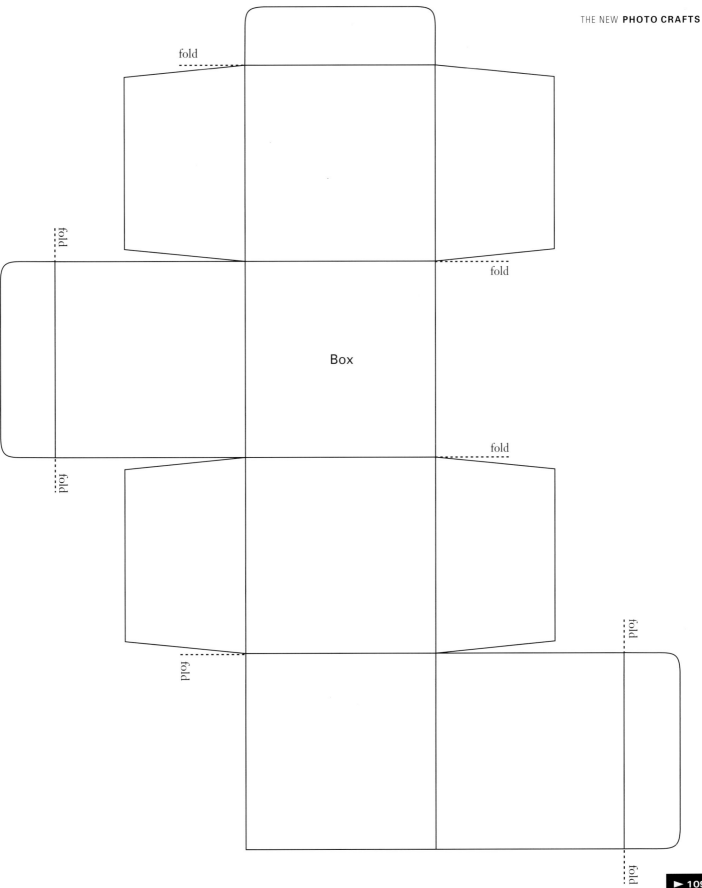

fold

fold

fold

fold

fold

fold

fold

Box

Floral Glass Coasters

DESIGNER: **KIM TIBBALS-THOMPSON**

A soft, springtime feeling is evoked by using a closeup shot of a sprig of delicate flowers, vignetted in white. The special effects available in computer graphics software can make your images even more effective.

Instructions

1 Scan your photo (or have someone scan it for you) using a resolution that is one-half that of your printer and a color monitor setting that produces an optimal screen image (use 16 million for the best color representation on the screen).

2 Crop or scale your image to a 3-inch (7.5 cm) square.

3 You can print this image as is or alter it in a variety of ways. The sample shown uses a white square vignette to fade the outer margins and bring focus to the center of the image. The options you have available will depend on the software package you use.

Another possibility is to overprint the image with text or a simple graphic shape, in color(s) or in white (called a reverse).

4 Print the image (use a color laser printer if at all possible, or consider working with a black-and-white image and printing it on a black-and-white laser printer). Trim the printout to a 3-inch (7.5 cm) square.

5 Clean the glass squares on one side. Sandwich the two pieces of glass with the image between them and the clean surfaces of the glass facing the image.

6 Peel back the adhesive protection strip of the copper foil tape about 2 inches (5 cm), and place the cut end of the tape on the center of the cut edges of the sandwiched glass, so that an equal amount of foil tape will extend onto the top and the bottom of the coaster. Continue peeling back the protection strip, wrapping the tape along the cut edges of the sandwiched glass and around each corner, and finally lapping over the starting point by $\frac{1}{4}$ of an inch (6.25 mm). Align the tape here for a perfect meeting. Trim the excess foil tape.

7 Burnish the edges using your fingers first, then a burnisher. To insure good adhesion, fold down the tape onto each side of the coaster and burnish well.

8 Apply the cork or rubber pads to the back side of the coaster at the corners.

9 Clean the front and back with glass cleaner. Never immerse the coasters in water.

Materials
(FOR 1 COASTER)

2 squares of single-weight glass, 3 inches (7.5 cm) each

13 inches (33 cm) of copper foil tape, $\frac{1}{2}$ inch (1.25 cm) wide (available where stained glass supplies are sold)

4 self-adhesive cork or rubber pads, $\frac{1}{4}$ to $\frac{1}{2}$ inch (6 to 12 mm) in diameter

Photograph or digital image

Tools

Personal computer with a printer, and a software graphics package

Scanner (or access to a scanner)

Scissors

Burnisher (the plastic handle of a kitchen spatula works well)

Glass cleaner and towels

Pressed Flower Bookplates

DESIGNER: **SUZANNE TOURTILLOTT**

Because book lovers love to loan books, be sure to use a bookplate as a lovely reminder to the borrower. In this design, the naturally elegant form of the flower needs no additional decorative treatment.

Materials

Fresh flowers, grasses, or leaves

Blotting paper

Full sheet of adhesive label stock, 8 $\frac{1}{2}$ x 11 inches (21.5 x 28 cm)

Microcrystalline wax (optional)*

Tools

Computer with plenty of available (free) memory

Scanner (or access to a scanning service)

Printer (inkjet or color laser)

Craft knife or rotary paper cutter

Metal ruler

Microcrystalline wax may be ordered from:

Light Impressions
P. O. Box 940
Rochester NY 14603-0940

(800) 828-6216
www.lightimpressionsdirect.com

Instructions

1 Carefully put the fresh flower between two sheets of blotter paper, and press under a heavy weight until thoroughly dry. This may take a week or more, depending on the thickness of the flower's parts. Store any extra dried flowers flat in a folded envelope made of waxed paper.

2 The bookplate's final size is 2$\frac{1}{2}$ x 2$\frac{1}{2}$ inches (6.25 x 6.25 cm). Launch the image software program, and set up a new file. You'll be printing multiples of the design onto the paper—three across and four down—for a total of 12 bookplates per sheet of label stock.

If your computer doesn't have enough memory for this, print out all the single bookplate designs on plain paper. These can be cut to the right size, then copied all together onto the label stock.

3 Access the scanner. Scan the flower at a resolution equal to one-half the printer's resolution. For a 600-dpi color laser printer (I used one at a local copy shop), scan at 300 ppi. Save the scan as a TIFF file format, naming it with an appropriate name. You can have a scanning service do this for you.

4 Using the screen ruler as a guide, center the scanned image in the upper lefthand corner of the canvas area. Using the text function, type a legend, such as *From the library of* or *Ex Libris*, and your name. Move the text to the desired position within the 2$\frac{1}{2}$-inch- (6.25 x 6.25 cm) square bookplate area. Merge the layers, if that is an option, only after the design is finalized. Save as a TIFF file.

5 Select the image (and the text, if it is still a separate, unmerged element in the design) and duplicate it. Move the duplicate to its correct position, to the right of the first design. Duplicate these repeatedly, until you have 12 evenly spaced bookplate designs on the page.

6 There are two ways to get the final product. When using an inkjet printer, you can print out the design directly onto the label stock. If using a color laser printer, you may need to print first onto standard paper stock, then photocopy the designs onto the label stock; sometimes the heat of a laser printer is too high for the adhesive label material.

7 Using a metal ruler, lightly mark in pencil the cut lines at all four edges of the paper. Use a craft knife and the ruler, or a rotary paper cutter (available to use free at some copy shops) to cut the stock down to the final bookplate size.

8 If available, apply a small amount of protective microcrystalline wax with a clean, soft cotton cloth. This wax protects paper from fingerprints and abrasion.

The Secret Ingredient Greeting Card

DESIGNER: **ROBYN ROSENKRANTZ**

Designer Robyn Rosencrantz cleverly blended several elements together to create a remarkable greeting card—a gift in itself. The photograph and the embroidered ribbon fragment from India, a recipe for Indian Chai Tea—even a tiny packet of fragrant cardamom seeds—stimulate the senses. Start with a recipe, a poem, or a story about the photo you're using. Choose the rest of the "ingredients" for your card with an eye for something funny, unusual, or sentimental.

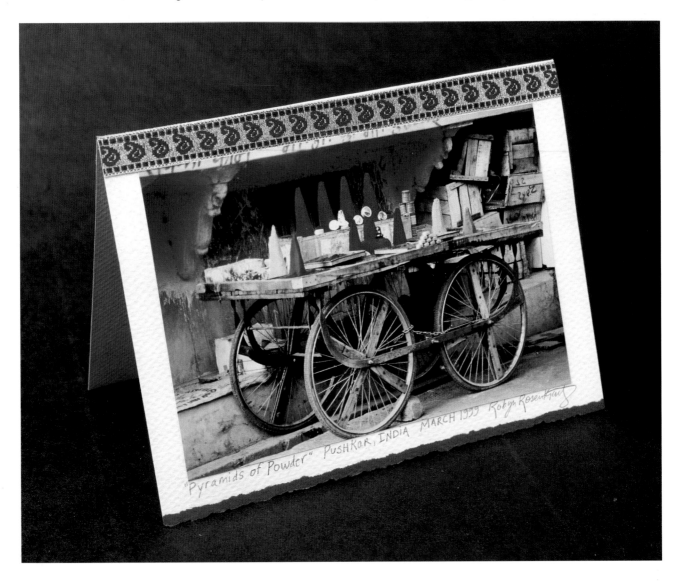

Instructions

1 Image software often comes with card templates that have preset attributes, such as page size and orientation. If you don't have templates, set up a new file in the image or word processing program you like. Type the information that will be printed on the back of the cards. Try an informal-looking typeface that is easy to read; reserve ornate typefaces when you are using a few words at most. The cards come flat and can be easily fed through most printers; black ink looks best. Before you run a card through, make a test print on text-weight paper to be sure you have the correct margins set. In this example the recipe was printed on the back of each card before attaching the photographs.

2 Fold the card along the score line or score it yourself at the halfway point, using the tip of a bone folder. Leave the inside of the card blank for a handwritten message.

3 Decide where you'll place the photo print on the front of the card, to get the feel of laying the photo down straight and centered. Then turn the photo over and put a self-adhesive photo square on each of the corners. Carefully put the photo into place on the card, making sure it is centered. Put a piece of clean paper over the photo and press down firmly on each of the corners.

4 Use a sharpened pencil to write your title, the full date that the photo was taken, and your name directly under the photograph. Titling is fun and adds an extra personal touch; the first title that comes to mind is often the best one.

5 Along the top edge of the photo you can put a piece of fabric, ribbon, or even sparkles, to dress it up. For fabric, adhere it with a hot glue gun. First measure the fabric and cut it to size, then center a small amount of hot glue on the back of the material so it doesn't ooze out onto the photo. Stretch the piece of material firmly into place and quickly press it down. If you want to use colored sparkles, put a little glue directly onto the card and sprinkle the sparkles. Let the glue dry completely.

6 For the "ingredient", put a few seeds, a bit of spice, or a little trinket into a tiny clear plastic envelope (see inset). Fold the top down twice, and use a tiny sticker or a stapler to close it. Apply a small dot of hot glue to the card—not the envelope— and then stick it alongside the text that was printed on the back of the card.

7 When giving the card as a gift, it's a good idea to put the finished card and the envelope inside a clear plastic bag to keep it clean. Seal the bag with a piece of clear cellophane tape, your favorite stickers, or a plain white address label sticker.

Materials

Blank greeting cards, flat and scored, with or without a colored deckled edge

Envelopes to match

Favorite photograph

Acid-free adhesive

Clear, self-adhesive photo corners

Ribbon, fabric, or sparkles

Sharpened pencil

Clear plastic bags (readily available in craft stores)

Tiny stickers (optional)

Tools

Computer

Printer

Hot glue gun or craft glue

Bone folder (optional)

Stapler (optional)

Recipe for Indian Masala Chai

My favorite song in India was "Chai, Chai, Chai, Chaiya, Chai!" I hope you enjoy a cup of hot or cold chai with a good friend, over inspiring conversation, or in sweet silence.

2 cups water
1 cup whole milk
sugar or honey to taste (for real authentic chai make it super sweet)
3 or 4 cardamom pieces - crushed but not powder (included with card)
3 teaspoons of loose black tea

Mix water, milk, sugar and cardamom in a pot. Bring to a boil. After it boils add tea and turn off flame. Cover the pot with a lid and let it sit for 5 minutes (or check color to your liking). Strain and enjoy! Double the recipe and drink in tall glasses over ice or refrigerate a batch for another day.

Other Masala ingredients are cinnamon, pepper, nutmeg, cloves, mint, anything goes! Fresh ginger gets added after boiling. Try one Masala spice at a time or mix them together. Creativity tastes great!

Bright Blue Gorilla photos (c) 1999 Robyn Rosenbrantz
To order cards or hear Gorilla music www.BrightBlueGorilla.com

Wilderness Hike
Digital Photo Journal

DESIGNER: **JILL TIMM**

Materials

Original photos

Heavy-weight paper for the pages

Linen thread or other very
    strong, heavy thread

Book board, or double-weight
    mat board, for the cover

Paper or fabric for covers

PVA glue

Ribbon, cord, and trinkets to
    decorate cover

Tools

Pencil

Scanner

Computer

Color printer

Ruler

Paper cutter or craft knife

Electric or hand drill,
    with $^1/_{16}$-inch (1.5 mm) bit

Scrap mat board

Strong clamps

Stencil brush for gluing

Clean scrap paper

Bone folder

Tapestry or other blunt-ended
    needle

The photos taken on this hike in the Rockies were later given a decorative edge treatment with image software, then printed onto watercolor paper with an inkjet printer. A simple Japanese stab binding will let you use heavier papers and folded out, panoramic pages.

Instructions

1 Select and organize the prints you'll be using. Keep in mind that you have the option to crop and resize them, which sometimes makes a not-so-hot photo look pretty good. In soft pencil on the backs of the prints, lightly write a number that corresponds to their order.

2 Scan the photos at 240 ppi. If you plan to resize to dimensions that are larger than the original, scan at a higher resolution.

3 The book's finished page size will be 5 x 7 inches (12.75 x 17.75 cm). Access the scans from within the photo software. Scale or crop the image to provide 1 inch (2.5 cm) of white space to the left, for sewing, plus a small white border around the other three sides. Touch up, add borders, or soften edges, as desired. Save the file.

4 Open a new file that is the finished size of the page: 5 x 7 inches (12.75 x 17.75 cm). Copy, cut and paste, or import, the image files into this page file. If using more than one image in your design, be sure to merge the layers (if that is an option) after finalizing the placement of the elements. Check your printer's page size settings.

5 If you are using large sheets of paper, orient the grain to run parallel to the book's spine before cutting it down to a size that will fit the printer. Print out all the images and text; see Printing a Digital File on page 99.

If you use a heavy-weight paper, such as 140-pound watercolor or card stock, score each page 1 inch (2.5 mm) from the sewing edge; this allows the pages to turn easily.

6 On a piece of paper that's the same size as the page's final dimensions, measure and mark for seven evenly spaced sewing holes. You can use any odd number for the sewing, but more holes will give greater stability to the book.

7 Collate all the pages. Put pieces of scrap mat board over the outsides, and put the paper marked for the sewing holes on the top of the stack. Use strong clips or clamps to hold them firmly together. Clamp them as tightly as possible, to reduce the possibility of burring. The holes need to be as small as possible, but big enough for the linen thread to go through twice. Drill the holes.

8 Using a strong linen thread, start sewing the pages from the middle hole, using a pamphlet stitch (see figure 5 on page 85), stopping at the hole where you started; do not go around the outside edge of the text block. Knot the thread over the center hole, then insert the needle through the center hole, hiding the knot within the pages. Cut the thread close to the knot.

9 Cut two covers, each measuring 5¼ x 7¼ inches (13.5 x 18.25 cm), which is ⅛ inch (3 mm) larger than the text block. Allow a bit more if you incorporated the deckled edge of the watercolor paper.

10 Cut out a piece of the decorative cover paper equal to the dimensions of the cover boards plus a 1-inch (2.5 cm) overlap in each direction.

11 Cut ⅞ inch (2.25 cm) off one end of each of the boards. These two pieces will be separated by a space equal to twice the width of the board; this allows easier movement of the cover.

12 Lay the cover paper face down. Mark the position of the boards lightly with a pencil, remembering to leave a space equal to twice the width of the board between the two pieces. (Hold two scraps of the board together, standing on edge, as a tool to add this space; it's easier than trying to measure such a small space.)

13 Use the stencil brush to apply glue to the board. Lay the board pieces on the paper, allowing for the space between them. Apply more glue to the paper that extends beyond the boards and finish covering the boards, bringing the paper neatly over the edges and corners.

14 Cover the inside of the boards with decorative paper that has been cut to fit the inside dimensions of the boards.

15 When the covers are dry, place the outsides of the covers together, then cover the front and back with scrap pieces of board. Put the piece of paper marked with the hole positions on top, and tightly clamp everything together. Using the drill, enlarge the second and sixth holes, so that they are big enough to hold a piece of decorative ribbon. You may need to burnish down the burr with the bone folder. Attach the cover onto the text block with the ribbon. Dip the ends of cords or ribbons in glue to prevent fraying.

DESIGNERS

KATHY ANDERSON has been a designer for four years. Her creativity and love for art and crafts has been with her since early childhood. She lives in the beautiful Northwestern United States, where color is abundant and influential. She has been married for 33 years, has two grown children, and two grandchildren. She loves camping, traveling, needlework, painting, and carving.

BETTY AUTH of Houston, Texas, is well known in the crafts field as an author and teacher. More than 150 of her craft designs have been published in national magazines, and she has made several television appearances, including those on Lifetime's *Our Home* and HGTV's *Carol Duvall Show*.

ROBERTA BATES has been a calligraphic artist and designer for 20 years, doing commission work from her home studio for companies all over the United States. Her love of sewing was recently revived when she received a new sewing machine as a gift.

PEGGY DEBELL creates one-of-a-kind wall pieces, clothing, and jewelry from just about anything, including burlap, tea bags, and bottle caps. Her creations incorporate her own photographs, which are transferred to fabric and/or paper. Her most recent works use familiar fragments from the everyday lives of women.

EVELYN ELLER has participated in many prestigious exhibitions, and her work can be found in museums such as the Whitney, the Queens, and the Brooklyn Museums in New York City, and the Smithsonian in Washington D.C. She has received both Fulbright and Yaddo Fellowships for her artistic endeavors.

DANIEL ESSIG lives in Asheville, North Carolina, where he is a full-time studio artist specializing in the book arts, at Grovewood Studios. He earned a B.A. in Photography from Southern Illinois University at Carbondale, and often can be found at the Penland School of Crafts—as student, visiting artist, and instructor.

Photographer **TONYA EVATT** has worked under contract for many outstanding publications and agencies, including *Forbes* magazine, *New York Newsday*, Sygma News Agency, the *Los Angeles Times*, and the Associated Press. Her photographs also have been published in magazines such as *Time* and *Newsweek*, as well as many other outlets worldwide. She obtained her B.F.A. in Photography from the Art Center College of Design in Pasadena, California.

POLLY HARRISON studied at the Atlanta College of Art. She weaves folded newspapers, discarded carpet braid, inner tubes, and discarded movie and video film into innovative baskets and three-dimensional wall hangings. Her work has been included in several major touring exhibitions, and for the past 12 years Polly has participated in South Carolina's and in Georgia's Artist-in-Residence programs in public education.

ESTHER HOLSEN is a graphic designer and weaver in Asheville, North Carolina.

DANA IRWIN works as an art director in Asheville, North Carolina.

Michigan artist and designer **MICHELLE KIERNAN** incorporates polymer clay, metalwork, precious-metal clay, and recycled found objects into her work. Originally trained as a musician, she still enjoys making music with her husband, composer Jim Johnston, in their home recording studio "The Digital Garden." She is currently serving her second term as the president of the Metro Detroit Polymer

Art Guild and is a member of the National Polymer Clay Guild. Her work is exhibited and sold nationally.

SUSAN KINNEY (B.F.A. in Sculpture/Ceramics and B. A. in Art History) is a designer who specializes in eclectic interiors, glass and clay jewelry, fabric and rug design, and computer-generated artwork of all kinds.

LYNN B. KRUCKE is a designer who lives in Summerville, South Carolina.

CONNIE MATRICARDI is a former art teacher who operates a small craft business from her home, making pillows that look like famous people, such as Shakespeare, Bach, and Poe.

JEAN TOMASO MOORE, a part-time multimedia artist, has been creating art in one form or another for as long as she can remember. She lives with her humble and patient husband in the beautiful hills of Asheville, North Carolina. Contact her at LeaningTowerArt@aol.com.

ROBYN ROSENKRANTZ, a California native, has lived and travelled all over the world. She is the creator of Bright Blue Gorilla, a company that strives to design original, inspiring, uplifting works. Whether it is designing greeting cards, recording original songs on CD, or performing around the world with her musical act, Robyn does her best to live each moment to the fullest. To hear Gorilla music, or to view Robyn's photo gallery, visit www.BrightBlueGorilla.com.

PAT SCHEIBLE's work appears frequently in Lark Books publications. She runs a decorative painting business from her home in Mebane, North Carolina.

LOIS SIMBACH is a Wisconsin native working for many years in fashion, textiles, and sculpture. She has an impressive range of freelance experience in costume design, theater, film, video, television, doll-making, and performance art, and presently lives in the high mountains of Western North Carolina.

TERRY TAYLOR's interest du jour is working with sterling silver and other metals in jewelry. He is a prolific designer and exhibiting artist, who lives in Asheville, North Carolina.

KIM TIBBALS-THOMPSON resides in Waynesville, North Carolina. She is a frequent contributor to craft books, and enjoys drawing, sewing, gardening, herbal-crafting, and broom-making. By day, she is a graphic designer.

JILL TIMM is a professional multi-media, instructional, and graphic designer for IBM since receiving her M.F.A. in Computer Graphic Design from the Rochester (NY) Institute of Technology. Listed in *Who's Who Among Young American Professionals* and *Who's Who in California*, Jill's work has been recognized in fine arts graphics (she's an outstanding serigrapher), photography, graphic design, and art direction. Her press is Mystical Places Press, and her work may be seen at www.mysticalplaces.com.

SUZANNE TOURTILLOTT trained as a photographer, receiving her M.F.A. in Photography from Indiana University at Bloomington. In her most recent incarnation, she is a book editor and a proud mother and grandmother, living amidst the beauty of the mountains that surround Asheville, North Carolina.

NICOLE TUGGLE divides her time as an artist, model, and marketing specialist in Asheville, North Carolina. Visit her web site at www.sigilation.com.

NANCY WORRELL is a widely published author and designer whose work combines her love of fibers with her needlework skills. Recent publications include P*aper Plus: Unique Projects Using Handmade Paper* (Krause Publications, 1997), and *Beautiful Wedding Crafts* (Lark Books, 1999). To see more of her work, visit her web site at http://hometown.aol.com/designsby.

ELLEN ZAHOREC is a full-time multimedia artist who works out of her Cincinnati, Ohio, home. She specializes in works incorporating handmade paper and collage. Her work has been exhibited internationally and is included in many private and corporate collections.

GALLERY

top: Janice Eaton Kilby
Asheville, North Carolina
Under My Skin
6 x 4 inches, closed (15.25 x 10 cm)
6 x 32 inches, open (15.25 x 90.25 cm)
Cyanotype on leather, fishing line

Photo by artist

bottom left: Peggy DeBell
Asheville, North Carolina
Closings
14 x 14 x 3 inches (35.5 x 35.5 x 7.5 cm)
Fabric transfer to vintage wedding gown, mixed media

Photo by Tim Barnwell

bottom right: Joni Ulman Lewis
Fredericksburg, Virginia
Summer Bestsellers
4 x 4 inches (10 x 10 cm) Books
8 x 8 inches (20.25 x 20.25 cm) Treasure boxes
5 x 5 inches (12.75 x 12.75 cm) Postcard sachets
Photo fabric transfer, color photocopies, mixed media

Photo by David Stover

top left: **Patricia Kennedy-Zafred**
Murrysville, Pennsylvania
Hopes, Dreams, Empty Cribs
19 ¾ x 25 inches (49 x 63.5 cm)
Photographs on acetate, photocopies,
fabric, mixed media

Photo by artist

top right: **Carolyn A. Dahl**
Houston, Texas
Eye Veils
28 x 28½ x ½ inches (71 x 71.25 x 1.25 cm)
Photo fabric transfer, mixed media

Photo by Maria Davila

bottom left: **Jean Tomaso Moore**
Asheville, North Carolina
Angel
25 x 15 x 7 inches (63.5 x 38 x 17.75 cm)
Photo fabric transfer, mixed media

Photo by Evan Bracken

bottom right: **Daniel Essig**
Asheville, North Carolina
Grandfather
4 x 6 x 1 inches (10 x 15.25 x 2.5 cm)
Wood, paper

Photo by artist

GALLERY

right: **Kathleen Campbell**
Sugar Grove, North Carolina
Angel of Technology
27 x 40 inches (68.5 x 121.5 cm)
Handcolored gelatin silver print
Photo by artist

bottom left: **Jill Timm**
Austin, Texas
Sky Islands
2½ x 2⅝ x 1/2 inches (6.25 x 7 x 1.25 cm)
Inkjet-printed photographs, paper
Photo by artist

bottom right: **Joni Ulman Lewis**
Fredericksburg, Virginia
Team
16 x 18 x 4 inches (40.5 x 45.75 x 10 cm)
Photo fabric transfer, mixed media
Photo by David Stover

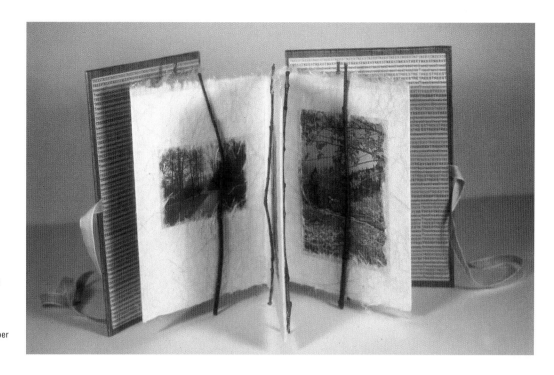

top: **Evelyn Eller**
Forest Hills, New York
Trees
11¼ x 7½ x 2 inches (28.5 x 19 x 5 cm)
Photocopies, mixed media
Photo by artist

bottom left: **Daniel Essig**
Asheville, North Carolina
Untitled
3½ x 2½ x 1 inches (9 x 6.25 x 2.5 cm)
Photograph, mixed media
Photo by Walker Montgomery

bottom right: **Sandi Cummings**
Moraga, California
Vessel
10½ x 8½ inches (26.5 x 21.5 cm)
Screen-printed fabric transfer, other fiber
Photo by Don Tuttle

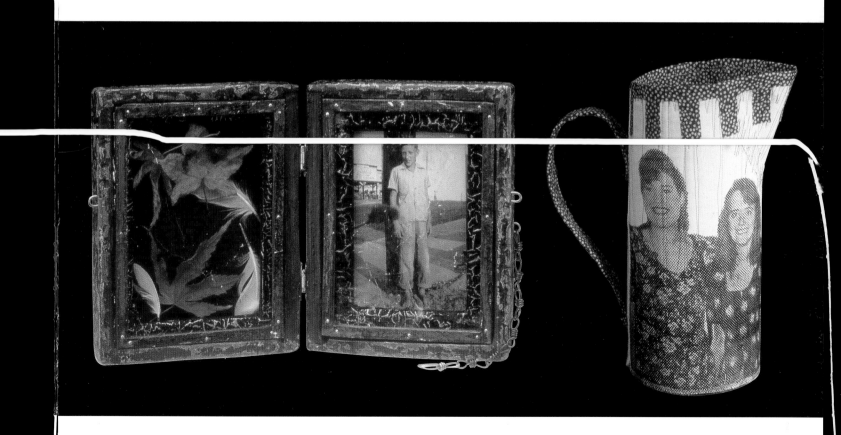

ACKNOWLEDGMENTS

No book was ever researched, written, and ultimately published, without the help of many, many people. Here are just a few of those who deserve recognition for their contributions to this project: Daniel and the whole late-night crew at Kinko's; Sir Speedy Printing; Esther Holsen and Jill Timm for their excellent observations on working digitally; Nancy Worrell's helpful hints on using photo transfer medium; Michelle Kiernan for her significant knowledge about polymer clay; Brian Caskey, for his awesome command of all things computer-related; the excellent and talented group of designers whose work is the backbone of this book; Harry Siegel, who always understands; and Deborah Morgenthal, whose guidance and sincere enthusiasm has been most valuable to me.

INDEX